So often in the line of min
I hear people ask the Fatl
to pursue this more. Wha
life of an individual? For m...,, ...g..... ....s......-
tion with where we are in our relationship with God. We want to
be motivated to pursue Him, yet we wait for some sort of visitation
from Father God to magically drop out of heaven instead of pursuing Him with the tools He has already given to us. Now, I am all
for heavenly visitations, but I also know there is wisdom in what
He is showing others in the body, especially the prophets. Loren, in
my experience with him as a friend and prophet, is one of the most
transparent, humble, and kind voices with his prophetic words. He
carries the heart of a pastor/father, someone who wants to see his
kids become all they were intended to be, while also carrying the
gift of the prophetic.

In this book, like all of his others, Loren exhorts the believer to
dig deep into the character of God. He encourages you to pursue all
the things you don't yet know about the Father while resting in the
total innocence of a child who knows he is loved and accepted just
because he belongs. This mind-set will catapult you into intimacy
levels with God so that your character will match your representation of who He is within you. *Yes, There's More* is a book about the
pursuit of love that will mature the character of the believer. Thanks,
Loren. Another winner.

—Trisha Frost
Cofounder (with the late Jack Frost)
Shiloh Place Ministries

One of the rarest things in all of Christianity is to witness a man
or woman of God who has endured decades of believing "for the
fullness of God" in his or her generation and not backed down no
matter the ups, downs, and turns the journey takes. Loren Sandford is one of these rare few who has stayed the course through the
years in pursuit of "the more." In this book Loren gives us a clear
vision of going deeper in God, coming out of slavery and into sonship, and receiving everything that God has for us. I am so excited
about the lives that are going to be transformed through reading

this book, because the truths contained in this book have radically transformed mine!

—**COREY RUSSELL**
DIRECTOR, FORERUNNER PROGRAM
INTERNATIONAL HOUSE OF PRAYER UNIVERSITY (IHOPU)

What refreshing simplicity! Simple obedience, not working up a feeling we call "faith." Relationship, not method. We can work no magic to obtain God's favor. He acts on our behalf because that's just what fathers do. Loren has coupled disarming innocence with deep wisdom in a way that will sink these and other truths into your soul at a deeper level than your heart has ever known.

—**MARK SANDFORD**
SPIRITUAL DIRECTOR, ELIJAH HOUSE
COAUTHOR, *DELIVERANCE AND INNER HEALING*

This book is for those who are truly hungry for the fullness of God to be manifest in and with them in their Christian life. *Yes, There's More* takes the spiritual and soulish blinders off the church and brings us to spiritual realities that must become His life in the believing ones today. Loren shares prophetic insight with true love and the transparency of the Father's heart in his life. I am on track with the realities of this extraordinary writing for God's kingdom now. *Yes, There's More* will impact those who are desperately hungry for the truth.

—**RICH HARRIS**
PASTOR, LIVING WORD MINISTRIES INTERNATIONAL

As a young pastor and prophetic voice in America, I wholeheartedly endorse R. Loren Sandford's new book, not only as a precious kiss from our heavenly Father but also a challenging trumpet blast calling us to purified ministry and living. With the Father's heart of compassion and tenderness, Loren issues a call to the body of Christ to return back to childlike innocence, where we receive wholeness and healing. For a generation of up-and-coming leaders who are hungry to see God move in America once again, this is a must-read.

—**JEREMIAH JOHNSON**
AUTHOR, *CHRONICLES OF THE UNKNOWN DREAMER*
SENIOR PASTOR, HEART OF THE FATHER MINISTRIES

Many of us have been praying for revival. Loren gives us hope for more than revival—and he shows us how to cooperate with the grace of God to return to a childhood innocence that makes it possible. This book will inspire you—and challenge you—to lay aside religious mind-sets and embrace the work of the cross and the blood of Christ. Rather than laying out another "formula," Loren offers revelation that motivates readers to pursue an intimacy with Jesus that will usher in a new move of God and stir a fresh hunger and thirst of a generation that has been disappointed by the modern church experience.

—**JENNIFER LECLAIRE**
NEWS EDITOR, *CHARISMA*
DIRECTOR, AWAKENING HOUSE OF PRAYER
AUTHOR, *THE SPIRITUAL WARRIOR'S GUIDE TO DEFEATING JEZEBEL*
AND *MORNINGS WITH THE HOLY SPIRIT*

Aha! I knew my longings for more had to be right—there is more! The kingdom of God is advancing! A shift is occurring from wanting to "be and do supernatural things" to having intimacy with the Father. Loren pens as a ready writer a "now" message about a new move of the Spirit that is an authentic, vibrant expression of the life of God that is clean, pure, and quenches the human thirst for such things. Those who have hungered and thirsted for a deeper revelation of who the Father is will certainly want to read and digest this book! Thanks, brother. Love your heart!

—**AARON EVANS**
SPEAKER, AUTHOR
KINGDOM CONSULTANT WITH THE EMERGING DANIEL COMPANY

In this book, Loren reflects what I believe is the heart of the Father for His people...more than many books I've read and messages I have heard preached in the last few years.

I count Loren as a good friend and someone I go to for counsel because I know what is in his heart. This book obviously reveals that desire in his heart and Father God's heart for the church as the Body of Christ here on earth not to get caught up in doing what they think Jesus would do, WWJD bracelets urging us onward to do, but to live so close to Jesus and to be so full of His Spirit that our everyday lives will ooze everything Jesus was while here on earth and can be now here on earth through his people.

Throughout the book, he urges us all to develop an intimacy with our Triune God that is the only thing that will bring enduring satisfaction to our hungry hearts.

This book is not only worth the time invested in reading it, but can change you as you read it. I highly recommend it.

—FRED WRIGHT
FOUNDING INTERNATIONAL COORDINATOR OF
PARTNERS IN HARVEST

William Booth, an 1800s Methodist Preacher and founder of the Salvation Army, stated, "I consider that the chief dangers which confront the coming century will be religion without the Holy Ghost, Christianity without Christ, forgiveness without repentance, salvation without regeneration, politics without God, and heaven without hell." How eerily prophetic and insightful his words seem to be for us today. Yet, in the midst of dark getting darker, the light of Christ is getting brighter. Jennifer LeClaire has refreshingly shed a spotlight on what the Lord is doing in and through many streams in the body of Christ. It only takes a few seeds to produce a great harvest and spark revival fires. Unconnected groups are spontaneously seeking the Presence of the Lord through corporate times of Worship, prayer, and fastedness. It's like a picture of many flickers of flames or candles across the land, yet when the Holy Spirit wind blows upon them, it will turn into one great fire of revival.

—DOUG STRINGER
FOUNDER AND PRESIDENT, SOMEBODY CARES AMERICA AND
SOMEBODY CARES INTERNATIONAL

YES
THERE'S
MORE

R. LOREN SANDFORD, MDiv

CHARISMA
HOUSE

Most CHARISMA HOUSE BOOK GROUP products are available at special quantity discounts for bulk purchase for sales promotions, premiums, fund-raising, and educational needs. For details, write Charisma House Book Group, 600 Rinehart Road, Lake Mary, Florida 32746, or telephone (407) 333-0600.

YES, THERE'S MORE by R. Loren Sandford
Published by Charisma House
Charisma Media/Charisma House Book Group
600 Rinehart Road
Lake Mary, Florida 32746
www.charismahouse.com

Unless otherwise noted, all Scripture quotations are taken from the New American Standard Bible, copyright © 1960, 1962, 1963, 1968, 1971, 1972, 1973, 1975, 1977, 1995 by The Lockman Foundation. Used by permission. (www.Lockman.org)

Cover design by Justin Evans

Visit the author's website at http://rlorensandford.com or http://newsongchurchandministries.org.

Library of Congress Cataloging-in-Publication Data
Sandford, R. Loren.
  Yes, there's more / R. Loren Sandford. -- First edition.
    pages cm
  Includes bibliographical references.
  ISBN 978-1-62136-980-6 (trade paper) -- ISBN 978-1-
62136-981-3 (ebook)
  1. Christian life. 2. Religious awakening--Christianity. 3.
Church renewal. I. Title.
  BV4509.5.S2645 2015
  248.4--dc23

                                        2014048010

First edition

15 16 17 18 19 — 9 8 7 6 5 4 3 2 1
Printed in the United States of America

To my father, who moved through the cloud before me so that I wouldn't have to. I wouldn't be who I am today without his influence on my life.

———— ◆ ————

CONTENTS

———◆———

FOREWORD

———•———

*Y*ES, *THERE'S MORE* is by far Loren's best work. In his prophetic teaching I have heard Loren say that modern prophets ought to be able to do as Jeremiah was called to do in Jeremiah 1:10:

> See, I have appointed you this day over the
>   nations and over the kingdoms,
> To pluck up and to break down,
> To destroy and to overthrow,
> To build and to plant.

To date, I haven't seen modern prophets doing much overthrowing, destroying, and planting of political kingdoms, but Loren dramatically fulfills Jeremiah's prophecy as he demolishes mental and cultural kingdoms and plants newly for the Lord. Chapter by chapter and page by page his brilliant analyses uproot and destroy our wrong ways of thinking and acting, and plant true intimacy in loving relationship with our Father.

In the first chapters he candidly exposes the self-centered, selfish ways of our culture that have crept into the church and into our lives, defiling our service to God with self-interest. Loren demolishes such ways and then kindly replaces them with loving service, not for any personal gains but simply to love the Lord of our salvation. In chapter 2 he ruthlessly reveals how we have lost our childlike innocence in fruitless quests and introduces us into the one true quest of our lives—to seek after and soak in God's loving presence.

In chapter 3 he uproots how our feelings have been conditioned into us as truth, thus falsely posing as the bases of faith, and how this has left us so often feeling guilty, frustrated, and depressed. And then he poignantly and powerfully replants us in the truth that real faith is simply obedience in trust of the goodness of our loving Father.

And so it goes, chapter after chapter.

There are so many "zingers" (sharp, concise statements of truth) on almost every page that you may wind up quitting the effort to highlight. Whole pages are turning yellow! And if, like too many of us, you are one of those who have built your life on some or all of the false premises Loren so efficiently uproots and destroys, you may begin, somewhere along in the book, to feel as if you are being flayed alive! But that will be the best flogging you've ever endured! Stay with it to the end. Your entire approach to life as a Christian may wind up being transformed into purer life and devotion and intimacy with God. That blessing is worth whatever humbling you may encounter before you get there.

Toward the end, in chapter 10, "A New Experience of Worship," Loren launches into what I know as his father is the passion of his life—what is true worship and what is not. That chapter is worth the price of the entire book. Loren is so passionate about worship and so aware of the many ways of worship that are not really pure expressions of love and thankfulness solely for the Lord's sake that he has composed the music and written the words of many of the songs of adoration sung in the worship services of New Song Church and Ministries, the church he founded and pastors.

This is not just another book. It is a transforming blitzkrieg in the warfare to establish the church and our lives where we belong—in simple, childlike innocence of devotion and intimacy with our loving Father.

—JOHN LOREN SANDFORD
FOUNDER, ELIJAH HOUSE

ARE YOU HUNGRY?

———— • ————

Percolating beneath the surface for a very long time, a sense of hunger for more—even a vague dissatisfaction with what is—has been developing in many of us who call ourselves evangelicals, charismatics, or renewal people. Over perhaps the last five years or more I've seen the hunger growing in the hearts of many Christians I've met in my international travels. Within a host of dedicated believers it has taken root. All of them are trying hard to feel touched despite the noise, hype, and supernatural promises being served up by well-meaning teachers with great ministries and powerful messages that, nevertheless, fail to satisfy the real hunger.

Maybe it's my background in counseling or as the son of John and Paula Sandford, who were pioneers in inner healing, that gives people a sense of "permission" to tell me what they've often been afraid to say aloud. Perhaps they sense something of the Father's heart in me. I hope so. But for whatever reason, they tell me, and I listen because I want to understand.

In the secret recesses of their hearts these precious saints question themselves: "Is something wrong with me? I'm just not feeling it. There has to be more than this." They long for something greater and deeper than what they've experienced, something more substantive than what they currently see and hear.

The truth is, yes, there is more. This book will restore a sense of intimacy as it points toward a simpler, more profound sense of connection with the Father. My hope is that it will remove layers of complication and striving and that readers will find a new and refreshing understanding of many passages of Scripture.

Obviously there are lighthouses of glory out there where the Holy Spirit's genuine fullness manifests on a regular basis—I am not ruling out those who feel complete satisfaction from their current experience with God and the level of outpouring in which they currently move. This book will speak as easily to the satisfied as to the dissatisfied. Rather, my goal is to lift one group to a higher place while helping the other group preserve the purity of its current experience. I would, however, be concerned for anyone whose heart does not hunger for more in their relationship with the Lord.

A shift is under way in the flow of the Spirit for those who can receive it. Some have felt as though they haven't been hearing the Lord as they once did or that they haven't felt His presence as they have in the past. This has been confusing to many. The truth is that things are changing, and we're being called into a higher place, a stronger place, a more stable place in the Lord. I'm convinced that from this will flow more powerful signs, wonders, and miracles than we have ever seen, but it does involve change, a refocusing of our senses and expectations. My prayer is that this book will help us understand the nature of the shift and open to us new and refreshing perceptions and experiences of the Father's heart.

Chapter 1

A TALE OF TWO ERAS

———◆———

In the fall of 1994 the Toronto Blessing had been going on for nearly a year, and the reports coming out of the meetings had finally overcome my skepticism. Realizing something of historic proportions had been loosed in an Ontario congregation then called the Toronto Airport Vineyard Christian Fellowship, I booked flights for January, and within a few months my associate pastor and I were making our pilgrimage into the bitter cold of a Canadian winter.

As a hardcore skeptic, my associate didn't believe that anything he had heard about Toronto could be genuine. But when we walked through the doors of that vast, inadequately heated exhibition hall, the power of God's presence blew him off his feet. For the entire week I saw him in just three modes: doing snow bunnies flat on his back on the floor, being carried to the hotel shuttle like a hopeless drunk, and hand-walking down the wall of the hotel to get to our room as he leaned into it to keep his balance.

Six nights a week, week after week, the revival broke

all the rules. My recording studio–trained ears couldn't stand the music blaring from a badly handled, inadequate sound system. Most of the preaching bored me to tears and went way too long—or it seemed that way, due probably to my own short attention span. Unlike so many other meetings termed *revival*, the ones in Toronto seemed to lack people with the gift of hype. No superstar leaders lined people up to push them down. No one screamed out messages that supposedly were from God, or even wore the requisite three-piece suit and tie. Over time everything from the sound system to the preaching underwent dramatic upgrades. But in the beginning things were pretty basic.

It therefore had to be God. People fell, shook, laughed, cried, were healed, and found refreshment. An army of ordinary people ministered in a spirit of sweet innocence night after night—and the impact was a floor carpeted with hundreds and thousands of people enjoying the simple ecstasy of the touch of God. I had been exposed to Charismatic Renewal all my life, since 1958, but never had I seen or felt anything like that. Likewise, never since 1995 have I received such pure and effective ministry anywhere I've traveled.

From all over the world people came by the plane-loads just to know the touch of the Father's love. Such was its reputation that the church, which came to be known as the Toronto Airport Christian Fellowship and, later, Catch the Fire, became Toronto's number one tourist attraction for a time. I made the pilgrimage myself from Denver, Colorado, two or three times a year just to be part of it.

Ministry was easy. We ministered to one another

and as part of teams with a clean and simple hunger for God and a childlike innocence, trusting and receiving freely from a Father we knew loved us. At times we felt like we were children again, being thrown into the air by Daddy or pushed high on a swing until that tickley *whoop-de-doo* feeling made us laugh. We weren't trying to make anything happen or force God's hand. We simply received what God was doing—and it was real. I would be remiss if I didn't give kudos to John and Carol Arnott for so faithfully and wisely shepherding that movement over the years. It had to be a daunting task.

Other revival streams sprang up in the years that followed. Despite being in other locations, they nevertheless were the same water in different flavors.

FADED GLORY: THE SHIFT

Then something changed. The focus shifted, not all at once, but so gradually that most of us didn't notice. We moved from purity of devotion to God and the freedom of mutual ministry by ordinary people to exalting our spiritual heroes—those we recognized as leaders in the movement. Many of us shifted from flowing easily in the Spirit to seeking ways to make the Lord move and to generating His presence with methods we had learned and knowledge we had accumulated.

Two meetings I attended—one in 2008 and the other in 2013—illustrate my point. In the spring of 2008 the Lakeland Revival was in full swing, with thousands of people gathering nightly in the Central Florida town for what was billed as a healing revival. Some leading voices had prophesied that it would be the one to sweep the world and change everything. My skeptic's smoke alarm started to beep, and I began to question how out of step I felt with so much of what I was hearing about the happenings in Lakeland.

My wife and I had been watching some of the meetings on GOD TV and questioned what it was that people seemed so worked up about. We just didn't sense the anointing that was supposed to be there, despite the television cameras zooming in on those behaving as if something great were being poured out. As we heard the prophecies from leading voices declaring this to be the great revival that would go around the world, we questioned whether something was wrong with us. We just didn't see it (although, to be fair, I have heard legitimate stories of healings people received there).

Finally, we decided in May to make the pilgrimage to Lakeland for a firsthand look. Although people told me the meetings were different in the beginning—and I have no reason to doubt that—what we saw after they had been going on for some time perfectly reflected what I know of television production and the camera's effect on viewers' perceptions. Having appeared before cameras on many occasions as a television host or guest, I know what they can do. And I saw it being done in Lakeland.

Perhaps three thousand people filled the tent. Up front, next to the platform, a few worshippers exhibited behavior consistent with manifestations of the Spirit. A few dozen crowded the platform to be as close to the music and anointing as possible. Nothing much seemed to be happening anywhere else in the auditorium. My wife and I felt even less of God's presence in person than we did from watching the meetings on television. The cameras, however, zeroed in on the few people at the front and, by doing so, created the impression for viewers worldwide that a great outpouring was being released.

People came from all over the globe to experience what the cameras told them was happening. I made a point of talking with a number of them. I wanted to get the pulse of these men and women who had traveled, many of them long distances, to attend the meetings. Most of them expressed disappointment in what they were finding and experiencing, some with bitterness and frustration. "Why did you come?" I'd ask. Consistently, with eyes downcast, they'd reply, "There's nothing where I live." Unable to find a genuine sense of the presence of God and freedom of the Spirit back home, they had come to Lakeland on the promise of finding the revival for which they hungered. Too many of them left disappointed.

Sensing something profoundly wrong in the meetings, I returned home to tell my people, prophetically, that the whole thing wouldn't last the summer. Some of them expressed real anger at my words, as if I were blaspheming a true work of God. But with every fiber of my being I knew what I knew. Less than three months later, on the sixth of August, it all ended when Todd Bentley, leader of the revival, departed and later was found to have been involved in serious moral compromises.

I have never forgotten the painful hunger carried by those who spent large sums of money to go to Lakeland in hope of finding an outpouring, only to experience disappointment yet again. Their words have echoed in my spirit ever since: "There is nothing where I live." On the down side, disillusionment can feed cynicism, even bitterness. There was plenty of that in the aftermath of what can only be called a betrayal. On the up side, however, tragedies like Lakeland sharpen our hunger for the real thing. Hurt has a way of carving deeper places in the heart, making it ready to receive a greater filling.

At the second event, in 2013, Heidi Baker was the speaker. Heidi is one of my favorite people and someone whose relationship with the Lord I crave for myself. Her Iris Global ministry of tangible expressions of God's love and compassion is changing Mozambique and other areas of Africa and the world. Her heart is among the purest I have ever encountered, so what I'm about to say brings no discredit to her.

Those of us who attended the meeting—my wife, people from my church, and my staff—all found it difficult to plug in to the worship. It could be that we were spoiled on the simple and innocent wonder of the early days of the Toronto revival and the anointing we enjoy in our own church. Part of it no doubt was the deafening volume of the music and the fact that we felt like the worship leader was screaming at us through the entire set, which was probably more a matter of style than substance. Although people around us were trying hard to act as if a powerful move of God was under way, we simply didn't feel it. Once more we questioned whether something was wrong with us. I still question that, but it doesn't weaken my point.

Heidi preached in her inimitable style, full of the humility, sweetness, and love that flows from her love affair with Jesus and the intimacy she enjoys with Him.

What struck me the most came at the end. "Don't look at me! Don't look at me!" Heidi pleaded repeatedly during the ministry time. A room full of dry, hungry people, desperate for a real touch from God, were looking to her to make it happen for them. They were making her the focus—but Heidi knew what they desperately wanted couldn't come from her. It would come only from Jesus.

Many years ago John Wimber, who led the Association of Vineyard Churches from 1982 to 1997, demonstrated once and for all that the average individual could minister signs and wonders. According to 1 Corinthians 12, every believer filled with the Holy Spirit has been gifted for supernatural ministry. Any one of us can heal the sick, pray for miracles, receive words of knowledge, and so on for ministry to individuals, for the edification of the church, and for the testimony of Jesus. The first years of the Toronto revival saw a wonderful innocence in which ordinary people ministered the extraordinary power of God with no single, discernable, great leader on the platform doing it for everyone. It was the era of the body of Christ, and Jesus alone got to be the superstar.

WHAT WE'VE LOST

In recent years, however, we've lost much of that early innocence as we have looked once more to the spiritual hero on the platform. Too many of us have turned away from seeking the simple purity of the touch of God and the wonder of ministering selflessly. Our focus has shifted. What we once did in innocence we now look for at conferences, where we expect to learn a method that will make it happen. Where we once hungered like children just to be with our Father, we now fill auditoriums seeking the supernatural from the superstar on the platform who we believe will "impart" something to us. We take home notebooks filled with instructions on how we too can do it. To be clear, I have nothing against learning more about ministry—I myself have a prophetic school—but such learning must never be allowed to obscure or replace simple innocence.

It often seems to me that the goal for some has subtly shifted from seeking intimacy to seeking to be supernatural. I've learned the hard way in a lifetime of exposure to the things of the Spirit that if your goal is to be supernatural, then you'll end up shipwrecked. If, however, your goal is intimacy with the Father and you hunger for His nature and character to be your own, then you'll end up being supernatural.

For many of us, what began with a selfless focus on delighting in the Lord has moved into seeking inner healing and other remedial spiritual "technologies" for all the wrong reasons. I call them "spiritual technologies" because they have been presented as methods and procedures to produce a desired result—if we could just say the right words or pray the right things or confess certain truths or address the right demons in the right ways, we could eliminate suffering and produce the happiness we desire. Do I just want to be happy, or do I want to be like Jesus? Do we want to prophesy for the Lord's sake, or because prophesying will make us part of the supernatural experience? Or, worse, because it will make us feel more significant, gifted, and recognized?

Is worship an entertainment event? Is it a song set of Christian cover tunes we heard on the radio? Is it an activity to make us feel something because we like the songs or the worship leader? Is it an activity designed for us to enjoy? Or is it meant to delight the God of our heart and put a tear in His eye or a smile on His face? Too many of us have lost our focus.

Do we want to do prophetic and healing ministry in the marketplace for the sake of the people we are ministering to, or more just for the thrill of doing it? Do we want it so we can feel like we're doing the latest "in" thing? In truth, how many of us are really very good at ministering to strangers on the street, anyway? I sincerely envy those with that gift! To be honest, I try, but I struggle with it every time I do.

This subtle shift in focus on so many fronts has created a growing sense of disappointment in an increasing number of people. The same sense of disappointment is gradually taking root in the so-called seeker-sensitive churches, which have not been part of the flow of revival. Even there, hearts are crying out, "There must be something more than this!" As 2013 came to a close, the youth group at our church began to see an influx of young people from a fast-growing megachurch in the Denver metro area, all saying: "I need more. I'm tired of the emptiness over there. It's not enough!" One young high schooler went back to visit the youth group there and reported to us that he'd been rebuked and told to stop talking so much about God because they didn't want to alienate anyone. It wasn't the first report like that we have heard.

We in renewal circles continue to fill auditoriums for

meetings and conferences. Anointed leaders with beautiful hearts preach great messages from the platform, but too much of the time something is missing—not as much in the speakers as in the people attending. I hear it everywhere I travel. I also feel the pressure of it personally when I speak from the platform. The expectation is that I do something to give people an experience or a personal prophetic word.

It seems to me as if an era is passing, even as it is peaking in numbers and prominence. A lot of good people are feeling this intuitively, neither knowing nor understanding what they're sensing. When I describe it, they say—and this is a quote—"At last someone is voicing what I feel! I thought there was something wrong with me!"

Excerpts from two e-mails I've received illustrate well what I'm hearing from a broad spectrum of people. See if something in you doesn't cry out "That's me!" when you read them.

The first is from my father, an icon of the Charismatic Renewal and a pioneer in inner healing and prophetic ministry since 1958. He wrote:

> It has grieved me when those of us who are in to inner healing have seen it only as something to return us to functioning, to having the good life. It's to impart, or release in people, the nature of God in Jesus so that Christians can manifest who He is to a troubled world. It's not even just to have a good character, but that God's character may shine through us for His sake, not ours. I hope you are right, that the new move is starting,

which is really the old. Revivals in the Second Great Awakening used to create vastly changed character; now too often they only make us feel good—while we go right on sinning. You could not believe how many spiritual leaders I have ministered to who have fallen morally. People need to see and know, not just for renewed hope but for calling, to let Him become their character of righteousness.

The second one came from a colleague in ministry in a different part of the country, someone who also experienced the wonder of the Toronto Blessing. This person wrote: "I'm 'sick' of all the me/I-focused 'worship' music and the whole 'me getting my feeling' emphasis, along with all the hoops to keep jumping through, along with the latest 'prophetic' word/vision stuff—and not to leave out the 'alignment' movement. More hoops! There I said it! It is time to get back to the Word, Christlike character, and the Great Commission and kick all the latest charismatic-gimmick hoops aside. Isn't it time to seek the genuine blessings of the Spirit and thresh out the chaff?"

What we once did in innocence, obeying the sweet moving of the Spirit, we now make into methods, structures, impartations, and alignments. But Jesus said, "Truly I say to you, unless you are converted and become like children, you will not enter the kingdom of heaven" (Matt. 18:3). There's the secret!

Getting to the Root of the Issue

I grew up in the great Charismatic Renewal that revived people in every major denomination and connected them for the first time with the living Christ. I was seven years old in 1958 when my parents received the baptism in the Spirit and became international leaders in the movement. Since then I've been touched in some way by every move the Spirit of God has sent to bless and energize His chosen ones—and I have seen every one of them inevitably fade. In movement after movement God poured the fine wine of heaven into a flawed cultural vessel that eventually leaked it away until it was either diminished or gone, or people simply mishandled it until one day the wine had lost much of its savor.

It's the vessel we baby boomers constructed so long ago, the foundation for which was laid by our fathers and mothers in the faith before us. Both in and out of the church we created and catered to a culture focused on self-fulfillment, prosperity, getting a blessing, having an experience, and being fed and touched personally and individually. We became a me generation, the opposite of a culture founded on the selflessness of the cross, which should have been the one imparted to us. We then passed our sick cultural orientation on to our children, who now suffer for it.

Conditioned by the culture we created, we gravitated toward teachings that taught us how to personally prosper, receive a blessing, experience the supernatural, and heal the pain our self-orientation inevitably produced. In too many cases we ended up with a faith focused in the wrong place—sometimes subtly and in some cases rather blatantly, but always self-serving.

Worship became an individual experience to receive and enjoy rather than a corporate offering rising as a pleasing aroma to God for His sake. Inner healing became less a tool for making us whole so that we could give our lives away selflessly in the service of others and more a means of relieving our pain so we could be happy. Prophetic ministry too often gravitated toward flattering words of great destinies reflective of the content of the hearts of the people it addressed rather than life-changing truth from God's mouth. We began to attend conferences for the big names on the speakers' roster, hoping the anointed ones would spark life in us and impart something that would give meaning to our lives or catalyze a supernatural experience in us.

WHAT'S THE REMEDY?

Jesus, however, came to reveal the nature and character of His Father: "He who has seen Me has seen the Father" (John 14:9). In the heyday of the Toronto Blessing, and in the years before it, we experienced wonderful revelation from great men such as Jack Winter and Jack Frost, who convinced us in no uncertain terms that the Father loves us. They brought healing to a generation wounded by the fatherlessness that grew from our culture of self. They fulfilled their callings well, but theirs was necessary remedial teaching, focused on receiving something from our heavenly Father to repair damage, heal hurts, and fill a deficit. Nothing wrong with that! But it was only part one of a two-part thrust of the Father's heart.

Too many of us wrongly injected that good teaching into our self-centered frame of reference. Too many of us camped on "Father loves me!" and there it ended as the wine leaked away through holes in the flawed vessel of our cultural construct, leaving us dry, hungry, and dissatisfied. It wasn't that we tried to put new wine into old wineskins that burst. It was that the cultural wineskin was rotten from the start.

The answer to our hunger comes not from a focus on receiving from God, although we'll never stop receiving. We serve a giving God, a loving Father, and one of the highest forms of praise we can offer Him is to gratefully receive what He sends. A growing number of believers, however, are coming to understand that the balm to soothe our growing ache focuses not on what we are getting or receiving but on what we're becoming. It's about the impartation of the Father's heart, nature, and character in us until we truly can be called sons and daughters of God who, from the deepest reaches of the heart, radiate who our Father is. Therein lies the second part of the message of the Father's love.

John 1:12 says, "But as many as received Him, to them He gave the right to become children of God." Note the adjectival Hebraism that goes beyond mere genetic inheritance or the truth that we are created by His hand. In Hebrew linguistic usage, to be a "son of" or a "child of" something is to resemble that thing in a significant way. Romans 8:19 applies the usage as well: "For the anxious longing of the creation waits eagerly for the revealing of the sons of God." I see a developing movement focused on impartation of the nature of the Father in character, disposition, heart, and spirit. It is a time of conformity to "the image of His Son" (Rom. 8:29). It has nothing to do with religious legalism or performance and everything to do with transformation of character from the inside out until we have the Father's heart as our own.

God's heart, then, would be to move us in this season from the remedial to the transformational, from receiving to becoming, so that we could exude the nature of the Father and the world would see and know Him by what they see and sense in us. We're not living for an experience. We're living for oneness with our Father through our Savior Jesus Christ in heart, character, and spirit. There lies the substance we long for.

It leads to a greater intimacy with the heart of the Father through Jesus than we have ever known. It is the realization of Jesus's declaration that it is enough for the disciple to become like his teacher (Matt. 10:25). When people saw Jesus, they saw the Father. It must be so in us. In the midst of accelerating numbers of scandals and moral failings involving prominent Christian leaders, isn't it high time people saw the nature of the Father revealed in His sons and daughters?

What are we becoming? Signs and wonders are not the goal. They are the result. Well-being is not the focus but rather the outcome. Prosperity is not the pursuit but the gift of a loving Father and the fruit of integrity. Glory must not be the longing of our hearts. It is instead God's response to a people who have become intimate with Him at the level of heart and character.

Hear this cry! What I'm saying and the direction in which I'm pointing is more significant and goes deeper than many of us realize. Everywhere I go I hear it in ordinary believers and in a growing number of leaders and teachers. We're returning to the innocence, the wonder, and the simplicity of the cross and the selfless nature of Jesus exhibited there. It's a freshened hunger— and out of hunger great movements are born.

Chapter 2

THE SECRETS OF INNOCENCE

———•———

I long to enter all God has for me and for the body of Christ. I want to see the fullness of the baptism in the Spirit, with all the miracles and manifestations of God's presence that the baptism implies. I hunger for the sense of His presence so strongly that it buckles my knees. I seek the kind of intimacy with Him that draws me into His heart deeply enough to know what He knows, feel what He feels, and think what He thinks. I will, therefore, keep asking questions. I will continue seeking and knocking on the door of heaven because I've been given a promise that if I ask, He will answer, and if I knock, He will open (Matt. 7:7).

All my life I've asked how it was that Peter in Acts 3 could command the lame beggar, crippled from birth with leg muscles long atrophied, to rise and walk, knowing that when he seized the man's hand it would happen. How difficult for Peter did that seem? In reading the account, it appears to have been so very easy (and that was just the beginning!):

And all the more believers in the Lord, multitudes of men and women, were constantly added to their number, to such an extent that they even carried the sick out into the streets and laid them on cots and pallets, so that when Peter came by at least his shadow might fall on any one of them. Also the people from the cities in the vicinity of Jerusalem were coming together, bringing people who were sick or afflicted with unclean spirits, and they were all being healed.

—ACTS 5:14–16

"All" were healed—not just some, not occasionally, and certainly not with any apparent great effort. Peter did nothing more than pass by! The Scripture says nothing about him doing anything special or saying anything just right. His shadow alone was sufficient to heal. Where did that come from? How difficult was it? It seemed so simple.

Then we have the apostle Paul, as described by Luke in Acts 13:

When they had gone through the whole island as far as Paphos, they found a magician, a Jewish false prophet whose name was Bar-Jesus, who was with the proconsul, Sergius Paulus, a man of intelligence. This man summoned Barnabas and Saul and sought to hear the word of God. But Elymas the magician (for so his name is translated) was opposing them, seeking to turn the proconsul away from the faith. But Saul, who was also known as Paul, filled with the Holy Spirit, fixed his gaze on him, and said, "You who are full of all deceit and fraud, you son of the devil, you enemy of all righteousness, will you not cease to make crooked the straight ways of the Lord? Now, behold, the hand of the Lord is upon you, and you will be blind and not see the sun for a time." And immediately a mist and a darkness fell upon him, and he went about seeking those who would lead him by the hand.

—ACTS 13:6–11

Paul knew that his declaration would become reality, or he never would have opened his mouth to embarrass himself. Where did that come from? What kind of confidence is that? How would or could any one of us walk in that kind of power today? How could you or I enter that level of intimacy and experience of the presence of God?

I've seen many believers trying to exercise that kind of authority through declarations and decrees, but the fruit has been scanty, to say the least. If it doesn't originate with God, it just doesn't work. Frankly I am sometimes embarrassed at the empty posturing this often represents. It often seems like a lot of work and wasted energy aimed at attempting to make something happen, when God really isn't in it. Disappointment and disillusionment result in those who witness and receive this kind of ministry.

Make no mistake! I believe that God has promised us greater works than Jesus did (John 14:12), which include the works of the apostles. It just seems apparent that something has been missing for the majority of us.

The Futility of Guiltlessness

I've come to believe that the answer to these questions has much to do with innocence. I don't mean innocence as the absence of guilt, like when someone enters a plea of "not guilty" at a criminal trial. Nor do I mean sinlessness. For most of us this innocence is both simpler and more elusive than that. "And He called a child to Himself and set him before them, and said, 'Truly I say to you, unless you are converted and become like children, you will not enter the kingdom of heaven'" (Matt. 18:2–3).

We accurately define the kingdom of heaven as "the reign and rule of God realized on Earth." Because there can be no suffering in heaven, the coming of the kingdom of God on Earth spells the end of suffering. In the kingdom of God, as His power becomes visible among us, we experience the flow of His love and witness its tangible effects. His presence so encapsulates us that the substance of heaven becomes manifest here in our midst.

Unless you become like children, however, you cannot enter that place. Unless something in you as an adult changes—is converted—and becomes not like the adult you are but like the child you were, then you will fail to experience or see much of this.

I state again that innocence is not the absence of guilt. Striving for moral perfection may be a worthy goal, but none of us will ever achieve it in this life. An honest reading of the New Testament record reveals that neither Peter nor Paul had achieved guiltless innocence at the time they wrote their letters—and they knew it, just as they knew the righteousness of Jesus stood for them, imputed to them by and through the cross and resurrection. Their confessions of failure remain in print for all to see.

Jesus spoke of innocence possessed of a childlike quality. If you believe in the innocence of children, as in the absence of guilt, then I have to question whether you ever had children. (See my smile?) We're conceived in a world of sin and are then born into it. We sin from the first beats of our hearts in our mothers' wombs. Guiltless innocence will elude us all, whether young or old.

"Whoever then humbles himself as this child, he is the greatest in the kingdom of heaven," Jesus said (Matt. 18:4). A childlike "humility" factor is what I'm calling innocence. So what is that?

In innocence, or childlike humility, we cease guarding and protecting ourselves, laboring so hard to control what comes into us and out of us. In innocence, we no longer wrestle with every thought, emotion, or action that comes through us, and we remain largely untroubled by events that happen to us or around us. As children, unless we grew up in abusive homes, we rested in wide-open acceptance of what our parents or someone older told us, showed us, or gave us. In adulthood, as we accumulate life's hurts and experience the effects of a fallen world, we tend to lose this trusting acceptance.

At I write this, I have three grown children and nine grandchildren. I can confidently say, therefore, that I understand a bit about little ones. When a nine-month-old suddenly hurls herself backward, trusting that the adult on whose lap she sits will be alert enough to catch her, that's innocence and trust. Or call it faith—but the point is, she innocently rests in the certainty that she'll be caught and has no fear of testing it. My two-year-old grandson knows that he will never go hungry, although you'd never know it to hear him demanding food at the top of his lungs. He never really worries about a meal. He knows he'll get it. That's innocence.

THE DYNAMIC OF UNBELIEF

Jesus said, "Therefore I say to you, all things for which you pray and ask, believe that you have received them, and they will be granted you" (Mark 11:24). This would describe the relationship, in innocence, of a child to a parent. But too often we make an incredible labor of Jesus's simple statement, trying hard to believe that we've already received what we prayed for (even though we don't see it) so that we can receive it. That's neither trust nor faith but rather unbelief leading to striving and disappointment.

What parent would fail to answer a child's need just because that child had doubts? Isn't our Father better than that? The striving we adults put forth in an effort to move God to act constitutes the dynamic of unbelief. Here's how: because we don't believe the Father really loves us, and because even when we believe it we don't understand it, we think we must work some method or have a particular feeling to move His heart to act, as if He doesn't already want to act or love us enough to give us what we need. Too many of us have it all wrong. We have traded the life of the Father's love for a form of salvation by dead works and have sacrificed the relationship in the process. The issue is innocence and trust.

When my grandchildren were little, they cried and

pounded the tray on the high chair while their mother prepared their food, not because they didn't trust that she would get it for them but because she wasn't moving fast enough. They knew beyond a doubt that Mom would bring them their dinner. In childlike innocence we know and rest in the knowledge that Father God cares so much for us that He will never let us down.

Was this kind of unguarded innocence and trust in the Father such a significant part of the character Jesus imparted to the apostles that they could function in childlike innocence without adult control mechanisms to impede the flow? Could it be that Peter, Paul, and the others trusted as a child would trust and knew therefore when God was on the move in love through Jesus? Is it possible that they had learned not to hinder the flow by means of the controls, fears, and doubts that too many of us have in place? Is that why they didn't seem to question whether or how the power would move through them for signs and wonders but simply moved with confidence?

THE LABOR OF SO-CALLED FAITH

Many faith teachers I've encountered seem to want to make a huge labor out of it. They tell us to work at believing that we've already received what we've asked for even though it has not yet manifested. The truth is that this actually expresses unbelief in the name of faith. It puts the burden on you rather than on the Father who loves you. Innocence is a place of rest in knowing the Father's heart in the same way a child would know and trust the heart of a wonderful parent.

We don't have to work at making anything happen. We need to learn to rest in what Father God is doing now and has promised to do in the future because He's a perfect Father and we're His children. God will not hold His love hostage to the limitations of my ability to generate faith. Just as He did for Israel when He parted the Red Sea, God performed the most significant miracles in my life when my heart was filled with certainty that I had been abandoned and was on my own.

As long as control mechanisms, barriers, and self-protections lodge in our character, and as long as innocent and open trust is in short supply, you and I will not be able fully and experientially to enter the kingdom of God. We'll block it out and won't even be aware that we've done so. The fullness of the flow of love and power through us will be restricted, not because God shut it off (He won't do that), but because we won't be able to sense Him enough to move with Him when He moves.

It's not that God refuses to send the flow. He has never stopped and never will. The question is whether we'll be able to perceive it and rest in the same confidence a child holds that a loving parent will meet every need. This explains why Jesus employed the word *converted*, which implies a change that must happen in the heart of each of us.

As I said earlier, one of my favorite people is Heidi Baker. The reason for this is not that she delivers such intellectually amazing messages. It's because, despite her obviously brilliant mind, she speaks the most wonderfully simple words that never fail to inspire me. She and her husband, Rolland, oversee thousands of churches in and around Mozambique. They have seen so many signs and wonders that, in my opinion, their ministry could legitimately fall into the category of "greater works" as promised by Jesus in John 14:12.

There's an innocence about Heidi where God is concerned, a childlike rest in the goodness of the Lord. In most of the messages I've heard her deliver, it seems that in her mind when there's a huge need to meet, it's already done. You and I fret and worry. For Heidi, there may be thousands of mouths to feed and nothing to feed them with, but it's as if she's saying: "No worries; our Father loves us. He'll provide—so set the table, invite the people, and get on with it! God multiplies the food."

I've never seen Heidi working at some spiritual method. I've never seen her advocating a book on how to confess this or confess that or push this button or that button to get God to move. As works of the flesh, those things express unbelief in the goodness of Jesus our Lord. Heidi's just a child who knows her Dad and trusts Him. With her, miracles happen, people get raised from the dead, and the blind receive sight—all because there's something about her that understands how to receive in innocence.

Adults work at things. An innocent child simply receives what the adult worked for. With us, God is the adult. Jesus worked on our behalf. He earned what He loves to give away. It's up to us to receive it. A child eats and freely receives what Mommy and Daddy worked for. Jesus sacrificed Himself on the cross and conquered death for us in the same way that a loving and trustworthy parent does things for a child. We must receive the benefit in childlike innocence or we'll miss the fullness of it.

A KINGDOM PROMISE

"Then some children were brought to Him so that He might lay His hands on them and pray; and the disciples rebuked them. But Jesus said, 'Let the children alone, and do not hinder them from coming to Me; for the kingdom of heaven belongs to such as these'" (Matt. 19:13–14). The kingdom of heaven—it's the power and the flow of God's will done here on Earth and belongs to those with a childlike, trusting innocence. It comes to such ones as can receive it in that spirit.

In Bible culture, when a rabbi laid hands on a disciple, the people believed that something of the character and nature of the rabbi was imparted into the disciple. Jesus's disciples rebuked the children for coming to have Him lay hands on them because they didn't think children were mature enough to receive what He had to impart. In their minds this kind of transfer came only after training, teaching, labor, and growth. Yet here were these children, untrained, immature, and without intellectual understanding, coming to receive what Jesus had to impart.

In the face of the disciples' objections Jesus said the outrageous thing—that you will receive the fullness of what He has to give only if you become like these children: "Truly I say to you, unless you are converted and become like children, you will not enter the kingdom of heaven" (Matt. 18:3). You need a childlike sense of unguarded innocence.

Witness the questions people asked the apostles. For instance, the Philippian jailer cried out, "Sirs, what must I *do* to be saved?" (emphasis added), and Paul's answer revealed what he had come to know in childlike innocence: "Believe in the Lord Jesus" (Acts 16:30–31). In Jesus we abandon everything to Him and follow like children, unafraid of loss, because we know our Parent will certainly be there for us.

Before Christ's crucifixion, resurrection, and ascension, the sons of Zebedee made a request: "Grant that we may sit, one on Your right and one on Your left, in Your glory" (Mark 10:37). Hardly a child's petition! Here we have the cry of insecure adults vying for position in order to gain a sense of validation. Jesus responded by teaching them to be servants, to take the lowest place, the place of children unconcerned for rank or position. This leads to the kind of innocence I'm articulating.

I pray that the Lord teaches me to be as simple as a child, and that we as the body of Christ will learn together what it means to trust the power and love of God. I pray that we learn to rest in the fact that His love and power will flow. I long for the day when what is not consistent with childlikeness, what does not reflect trust, and what constitutes control will not get in the way. Innocence does not control, block, or impede the flow of His presence or power. It just receives. Many of us pray fervently for revival, but the problem isn't in the sending. It's in the receiving. We make it too complicated and block it out with our striving and efforts to make it happen.

"Truly I say to you, unless you are converted and become like children, you will not enter the kingdom of heaven" (Matt. 18:3). Jesus spoke of innocence, not the absence of guilt, but rather a quality of trust, receptivity, and rest in the faithfulness of a loving parent. I want to know that He will move through me for the sake of others. Jesus taught that the quality of knowing that I seek comes through the innocence of childlike trust.

When you lay hands on someone to pray for healing, must you possess special knowledge or training, some esoteric method you learned in a seminar or a conference, to see power flow and healing happen? Does it require that you do something magical or say just the right words? Must you somehow "channel" what God would send? Or is it sufficient to innocently trust that He will flow through you and all you need to do is let Him? Sin makes things complicated. Innocence makes everything simple. Learning can sharpen the gifts, but never let it chip away our innocence.

When I enter the room, my granddaughter, now age five (one of my five "grandlovelies"), looks up, breaks into a grin, and holds out her arms. I pick her up and we cuddle, tickle, play, and kiss. She's not writing a theology of her grandfather's love. She didn't study principles of how to approach and access Granddad's benevolence. She had no need to study a two-hundred-fifty-page book to learn how to talk to me. She does it naturally and freely because she trusts my love and knows she has permission to be herself. That's innocence, and it's in that kind of simplicity that we must come into the kingdom of God and all its power.

One of my grandsons, at age three, used to see me in the doorway of the house; shout, "Granddad!"; and run to jump on me like a chimpanzee leaping into a tree. He didn't have to spend one hundred dollars in registration fees and fifteen hundred dollars to fly to a distant revival center and rent a hotel room to hear somebody tell him how to receive his grandfather's love. He simply did it, unguarded and uncontrolled, knowing that my love was there for him to receive, free of any cost or pretense. That's innocence—and for the record, I would spend one hundred dollars on a registration fee and fifteen hundred dollars for flights and a hotel room if it meant I could find that innocence!

Jesus called us to this childlike relationship with Himself, but we grow up and become ever more dysfunctional until someone has to teach a class or preach a sermon to get through to us. Even then, it seems, we often miss it. Eventually someone will read the words of this book and experience a great revelation in freedom. They'll share it with others, and the words will be passed around, only to be sapped eventually of their meaning as adult minds and hearts process them into mere knowledge and method.

RECLAIM YOUR INNOCENCE

When did you begin to be on guard—if you are? When *when* did you lose your trusting, wide-open innocence that would have opened your heart and life to the fullness of the kingdom of God? When did you begin to control the flow? Perhaps you feel you must pay good money to go to serious counseling to relearn how to do what you knew to do naturally when you were a child. If that's what it takes, then get it done! Innocence is worth it!

When did innocence begin to be crushed? Was it when your earthly father broke a promise for the first time? Was it when your mother carried the discipline too far or punished you for something you didn't do?

Was it when Dad came home drunk and abused you and your family? Was it when you heard your parents fighting in the next room or when one of them left home and abandoned you? Was it when they told you that you were worthless or ugly?

In that hurt, did you begin to build a world of control over what you felt and what you would allow other people to see? In your need to protect yourself, did you build a set of prison bars around your feelings, restricting their expression in order to get along in the world, because you had learned not to trust all those sinners around you?

Those controls work against intimacy with both people and God, rendering you unable to trust either of them. Innocent receptivity to God's power and love gets lost as the power and love He sends must pass through your self-protective control grid. You can't just let the power and love happen—control gets in the way.

I know from experience the truth of this. For the first seven years of the Toronto Blessing I was a post, standing like a tree in a forest of fallen trees as others around me went down under the power. No matter how hard I tried or how much I hungered, I couldn't release control. It's not that God won't move. In fact, He never stops! His love and His nature are so great that He will never allow Himself to be held hostage by the human condition. In our dysfunction, however, we can become like the autistic child whose parents long to hold and love her, but she cannot or will not allow it.

When the blockage doesn't stem from old hurt, it could mean that it's coming from someplace else—sometimes it can be that we are trying to know too much. We believe we have to learn how to heal, how to pray, how to have spiritual experiences, and how to hear from God. At that point, "knowing how" itself becomes an obstacle when we move from "God did it and isn't that amazing!" to "I know a method that works!"

Paradoxically, knowledge that can and should enrich both experience and the effectiveness of ministry becomes the very thing that dries us up because we've taken control. We've ceased to be children receiving in innocence, who don't need to know and understand beforehand what we're receiving. "Surely I have composed and quieted my soul; like a weaned child rests against his mother, my soul is like a weaned child within me" (Ps. 131:2). This is where we need to be.

It's time for a baptism in the Spirit, a full-on visitation of power and love on us as a people, but it's also time to ask God to make us children again in innocence and trust.

Chapter 3

DO YOU HAVE THE
WRONG FEELINGS?

———◆———

This chapter could be an upsetting one for some. I seem to have a talent for doing that to people, but my heart is to set them free from bondages they often cannot see, many of which are found embedded in commonly accepted theologies and ideas prevalent in Christian circles. Unfortunately much that has been accepted as truth in the body of Christ has little real basis in Scripture. Predictably this brings disappointing results when the teaching fails to deliver on its promises. As you read, therefore, please hear the heart of the Father.

I have included substantial sections of personal testimony. Please bear with me because the stories illustrate the point. Some of you will discover another layer of the cause of your disappointment and frustration.

I was born a prodigy with a brilliant mind that was able to quickly absorb just about anything. I learned to speak long before any normal child should. Before the age of two I had the language skills of a child of five. I'm told that my father's seminary friends often entertained themselves by giving me big words to say. Imagine a twenty-month-old repeating things like "extraexistentialism"!

In those first two years I loved life. At a year and a half, full of laughter and ready for adventure, I figured out how to work the fire escape on our second-floor apartment, got out, and set out to explore our inner-city Chicago neighborhood on my own. Fortunately some honest passerby found me and returned me to my frantic parents. To save my life by reining in my sudden impulsive urges to dash off in unexpected directions regardless of danger, my parents bought me a harness and leash.

When I was eighteen months, my baby sister entered the world. I loved her and remember feeling profoundly disappointed when my parents told me I couldn't marry her. Full of love and adventure, life was good.

My world of light and life faded out when two things happened. I clearly remember lying paralyzed in my crib, looking up at my parents through a dark and cloudy haze in an unlighted room. Although my father was a seminary student, preparing for the ministry, he wasn't yet really saved, much less filled with the Holy Spirit. The apostate liberal school he attended did everything it could to destroy real faith in scriptural truth. Later in life I learned from my father about demonic attacks and how to deal with them, but at that point my parents knew nothing about deliverance.

As I lay there, helplessly immobile and tormented, I could hear them discussing in a seemingly detached way what might be afflicting me and wondering whether they should take me to a doctor. All I knew was that something had gone terribly wrong with me, and no one could help. Later, after rooting himself in the Word and receiving the baptism in the Spirit, my father taught me how to exercise authority over the demonic realm. But damage had already been done. From that point forward I knew I was pretty much alone in life when it really mattered. At the age of seven, innocently assuming that my experience was normal, I shared the details of these attacks with my Polish Catholic playmates. They told me, the Protestant preacher's kid, that I was being judged by God for not being Catholic.

The second incident happened during the same period of time as the demonic attack in my crib and carried with it a much more significant emotional devastation. While my father attended seminary during the day and drove a taxi at night to support us, we lived in a run-down, smelly, old apartment building in a bad neighborhood. The only children I could find to play with lived in a decaying, multilevel tenement building a block or two away. My mother called them the "roughie-toughies."

The front doors of the tenement faced outward, and the back doors opened onto fire escapes that led down to a square enclosed by the buildings and filled with garbage cans tucked under the rusty iron steps of the fire escapes. This arrangement formed the dark boundaries of the only playground available to the children of the tenement residents.

My precocious mastery of language caused the uninformed to assume I was much older than I actually was, and the tenement kids were no exception. One day I mounted my tricycle to pedal my way to the "roughie-toughies," hoping to find playmates and feeling very certain that everyone liked me. Always fascinated with small things, I found along the way a smaller tricycle, traded my big one for the smaller one, and pedaled into the tenement. The result was a nightmare. From the shadows behind garbage cans under fire escapes came mocking voices calling out: "There's the baby! He's really four, but he thinks he's two! He just wants to be a baby!" I never saw their faces.

Desperately wounded and full of fear, I left the tricycle and ran home in tears to tell my mother what had happened. Her response set a pattern that stayed with me and warped my perceptions of life and God for five decades. "You just shouldn't feel that way," she said. But I did. To her credit, she thought she was helping, but from that point on I knew myself to be fundamentally defective at a foundational level. I didn't have the right feelings.

Then came the condemnation for losing my tricycle. In our poverty, any form of loss cut deeply. Although today, as an adult, I understand my parents' dismay, the message they unwittingly sent me at the age of two served only to establish my assessment of myself as a fundamentally flawed human being. Together with the demonic attacks I suffered, the experience brought down a curtain of darkness over my life and spirit that formed a prison I could not fight my way out of for decades to come.

As I grew older, the rejections began to multiply. No matter what I did, I could never be good enough or right enough to be accepted and included. With that dark cloud of negative expectation hovering around me, most people, especially my peers, didn't want me around. I was too weird, too different, and too disconnected from the normal flow of things.

Acceptance, I soon learned, came only when I could dominate others, become a leader, and create the flow myself. So I formed a neighborhood gang that shoplifted from every store that sold candy or balsa wood gliders within a mile of home. We soaped windows, peed in gas tanks, rang doorbells, and egged houses— all because I knew I was just "wrong" as a human being and there was nothing I could do about it.

My father, a truly righteous man, played with us children, read us stories, and took me on hikes in the woods, but he didn't know how to listen to or understand a child's emotions. Because his own mother had worked him hard as a child, he had trouble understanding which chores were age appropriate and which weren't. He therefore had a habit of giving me jobs to do that were too big for me (age inappropriate)—and when I failed, the condemnation came down that somehow I was just lazy, because if I had really wanted to do the job, I could have. Once again I knew myself to be defective. On the up side, I did learn to work hard.

Inevitably depression set in just about the time my parents received the baptism in the Spirit (1958). They began to move in all the good things the Holy Spirit brought, but in those early years they also soaked up some of the bad teaching—the unbalanced and unbiblical doctrines that grew out of it. When I tried to express my hurt and depression because I couldn't understand the hurt I carried, they responded, "You just shouldn't have those feelings," and told me to praise God for all things. (See Ephesians 5:20.) On balance, that was a good teaching, but when I expressed discouragement and tried to explain the obstacles I faced and the failures I suffered, they said, "Well, your life just isn't like that!", as if I were completely mistaken in my perceptions of reality. We were a good and solid family, but we weren't perfect!

Why do I share all this and spend so much time on my own personal testimony? Because although your story probably doesn't take the same form as mine, the nature and effect of it may have been similar. Too many of you received the same set of messages I did, and you adopted the same set of ungodly beliefs about yourselves and about life. This has rendered you vulnerable to forms of supposed revelation that actually lead into new forms of salvation by works through human striving.

For me, in those vulnerable and formative years of my life, it seems that as a family we had no adequate grid through which to process the truth of the Father's love. Consequently, by the time I reached adulthood, I had become convinced that God couldn't bless me because I had all the wrong feelings.

LEARNING A DIFFERENT REALITY

Enter faith teaching and prosperity doctrine. Just as I came of age, the Charismatic Renewal became saturated with an unbalanced message that seemed to equate faith with a set of feelings. I was told repeatedly by many well-meaning people that my emotions were all wrong and that as long as I felt that way, hurting and depressed, I was expressing unbelief. It implied, at least to me, that if you couldn't generate some mysterious quantity of belief in your heart, then God could not or would not bless you. To counter this, we were taught to confess this and confess that, as if our words could create the reality that our inward faith could not. Most of it stemmed from a basic failure of real trust at a childlike level. At root, the question wasn't, "How can I trust the Father who loves me?", but rather, "How can I get God to move on my behalf?", as if He really didn't want to and had to be coerced.

Because I suffered from depression and couldn't feel all those positive, joyful emotions no matter how hard I tried, and because I could not generate an emotion of expectation that God would do great things for me, I believed God couldn't favor me. Everything I heard all around me in renewal circles reinforced that sense. Well-meaning Christians told me that if I had the wrong feelings, God's work in my life would be restricted. I would reap destruction.

After seminary I planted my first church. On the good side, that church became self-supporting very quickly and paid me a full salary. On the down side, I drew a very broken group of people who constantly attacked and criticized. They came because I planted the church out of my counseling office when I was working for Elijah House, my parents' international healing ministry, and very few of those people were emotionally healthy.

Under the pressure of the constant criticism that flowed from their dysfunctions, I sank yet deeper into depression. When I tried to share that and work it out with my parents and family, who by now were the world standard for inner healing, they didn't understand. They told me what I had always heard: "You just shouldn't feel that way." If I had the wrong feelings, the blessing of God would be limited. In my despair I actually came to believe emotionally that all the good things in my life, from my home to my wonderful children, had come because God loved and favored my wife, not me. Ever positive and upbeat, she had the right feelings, and I didn't.

This was the dark place where I lived imprisoned for more than five decades, believing that because I couldn't seem to feel the way I was supposed to feel, God withheld blessing. It would be difficult to express how much energy I invested in trying to push all that hurt aside so I could keep it under control, function in life, and do what I had to do.

Inevitably the day came when my pain bucket overflowed and I could no longer control it or hold it in. After I spent a couple of days watering the carpet with my tears at a conference in Toronto, my friend Fred Wright, founding coordinator for the Partners in Harvest church network and a wonderful pastor, put me in touch with Chester and Betsy Kylstra of Restoring the Foundations. With their help I began to dispense with the ungodly beliefs I had lived with all my life, and I finally broke free.

Looking back, I realized that my feelings had never had anything at all to do with God's ability or willingness to bless and prosper me. What counted was His love, not my emotional condition or any failure of mine. While the body of Christ seemed to equate faith with a set of feelings—and sent the message that God couldn't bless you if you didn't confess positively and have the right emotions—I realized that my Father God had given me a wonderful wife, even in the face of my failure. Together we had produced three awesome children, all of whom serve the Lord today together with their spouses. We bought our first home because of a miracle of provision. That led to our second home and then to our third where we now live in Denver, Colorado.

I planted our first church in the panhandle of Idaho and pastored it for eleven years. Without any help from the denomination we were part of, that church became self-supporting and paid me a full-time salary within two months of our first service of worship. In fact, the denomination branded my original proposal to plant a church as "frivolous" and refused to aid us in any way. God did these things for me in spite of my emotional condition of unbelief.

A year after the first service of worship, the church bought ten acres with a house and a barn. After removing four truckloads of old manure from the floor, we moved our services into that humble structure. Four years later, in 1986, we built a four-hundred-seat architectural wonder on that property for just $400,000—at a time when it should have cost $700,000 and we didn't even fully qualify for the loan.

These miracles of provision had nothing to do with what I felt or didn't feel. God's love and favor would not be held hostage by my human condition. Through it all I confessed all the wrong things, felt all the wrong things, feared all the wrong things, and lived day to day in clinical depression. There are no wrong feelings in faith, only wrong actions!

I planted my current congregation in Denver as I was coming out of a very bad situation, arguably the low point of my life. Fourteen months on the staff of a Denver area megachurch had ended in disaster for me. I found myself rejected and maligned, and, moreover, the victim of a host of vile stories and accusations that had no basis in truth. Deep in depression and having no idea which way to turn, I felt I had led my family into a blind alley.

In the fourteenth month of my tenure there (June 1992) my wife and I traveled to Vermont where I was scheduled to speak at a conference alongside Francis and Judith MacNutt and Leonard LeSourd, iconic leaders in the Charismatic Renewal. Judith took one look at me and compassionately stated, "You're clinically depressed." She was right. Battered and deeply bruised, I could make no positive confessions no matter how hard I tried.

Once again our Father proved Himself bigger of heart than anything I might have been feeling or saying. I knew God had called me to plant a church in Denver, but in the face of the pain and opposition leveled at me, remaining in Denver was the last thing I wanted to do. While I was in Vermont, I told the Lord that if He really wanted a church plant, He would have to confirm it by providing me with three months' income up front at the rate I had been paid at the megachurch. Although nothing was said to the conference attendees, they began to give money, saying simply that the Lord had nudged them to do it. Before that conference ended, I had one and a half times what I had asked for.

Once more my emotional lack of faith failed to have the power to turn back the Lord's favor. He's bigger than that. He's better than that. His love passes understanding and will not be held hostage by my emotional state or my limited, fleshly ability to believe (or anyone else's).

Looking back on all this, and in no small measure due to the help I got from the Kylstras, I know beyond a doubt that faith can never be defined as a measurable quantity, so that if you have enough of it, then God has to move, and if you don't have enough of it, then He doesn't have to move—or won't. Can you imagine the God who defines Himself as love saying, "Well, you need five pounds of faith for Me to move, but you have only four and a half, so I can't do anything for you"? The real effect of my lack of faith was only to plunge me unnecessarily into depression.

THE REALITY OF FAITH

Faith lies in the act of obedience, in the position in which you place yourself in response to the call and command of God. Fear becomes unbelief and lack of faith only when acted upon. Depression constitutes unbelief only when you obey the urge to isolate from others, choose to abandon your calling in life, or both.

You might say, "I don't have the faith to tithe," but what you really mean is that you're obeying a feeling. The feeling isn't the issue. Lack of faith manifests, not in emotions, but in failure to take action in obedience. Faith lies in the doing.

The quality of my life and destiny in the Lord through all those years of clinical depression stood because most of the time I determined to refuse to act on fear, depression, and negative feelings. I chose instead to obey God no matter what I felt. Certainly I failed—and often— but God continued to bless me even when I stumbled.

I went to seminary after earning my bachelor's degree, and I was afraid that I wasn't intelligent enough, that I would fail, and that the money wouldn't be there both for tuition and to provide support for my family. But I didn't obey those feelings. Out of the depth of His loving heart God provided. I felt that my gifts would be inadequate for successful pastoring, that I would fail because of my defective nature. Try as I might, I couldn't generate all those positive feelings I thought I was supposed to have. But I didn't build my life and ministry around those failings. I obeyed God and put myself in positions in which He could prosper what I did. Unbelief lies not in the emotions but in the failure to move.

THE HALL OF FAITH: HEBREWS 11

"By faith Noah, being warned by God about things not yet seen, in reverence prepared an ark for the salvation of his household" (Heb. 11:7). I don't think Noah waited to experience some emotion of certainty about the ark before he started construction, or that he had a sudden uncontrollable inner urge to build a very large yacht on dry land far from the sea. What would the neighbors think? It didn't matter. Faith didn't rest in any feeling. It was in the doing.

"By faith Abraham, when he was called, obeyed by going out to a place which he was to receive for an inheritance; and he went out, not knowing where he was going. By faith he lived as an alien in the land of promise, as in a foreign land, dwelling in tents with Isaac and Jacob" (vv. 8–9). Did Abraham experience a sudden emotional compulsion to move? Was he delighted to do that? Leaving his ancestral home meant abandoning everything he knew: his family, his father's country, his heritage, and his inheritance. What God told him to do sounded like, "Sell your house and go live homeless for a while in a country where you don't speak the language until I tell you where to settle." How many of us would leap at the chance to do that?

Doubt. Fear. Uncertainty. Grief. All emotions Abraham may have felt. For Abraham, faith didn't consist of some mystical sense of certainty. It lay in acts of obedience, taking action in spite of feelings. Negative feelings didn't stop God from pouring out provision.

"By faith Abraham, when he was tested, offered up Isaac, and he who had received the promises was offering up his only begotten son" (Heb. 11:17). Try this: "I'm just *so* excited that I get to kill my son, my only son, and burn him up! *Yeah!*"

Some say Abraham trusted that God wouldn't actually ask him to do it. Not so. Nothing in the words of Scripture justifies that kind of a conclusion; everything in the biblical record leads us to believe Abraham stood poised to obey—so much so that to stay his hand God had to call his name twice, loudly, "Abraham! Abraham!" Faith lay in the doing regardless of his feelings. Abraham set his will to obey in spite of his inner state of being. God stopped him and brought glory and a destiny out of it.

The idea that feelings are truth and faith is a feeling is a massive deception perpetrated on us in recent decades to trap and imprison untold numbers of us in striving. It will set you up for the disappointment I'm addressing. It's time to break free and come to know the Father for who He really is. By means of this deception the enemy of our soul has sought to strip us of strength and turn us into an ineffective, weak, mood-driven, inconsistent, and powerless group of people the world cannot respect. Thus the gospel is neutralized.

SET FREE

I'm no longer clinically depressed. God has healed me of the roots of that dark state of being. I know beyond a doubt that I am not and never was defective, my sin nature notwithstanding. I'm gifted and chosen, not rejected. My emotions today are stronger and less controlled than ever, and some of them—a minority—are negative, but those feelings are neither right nor wrong. They just are, and I'm free of their domination.

In my college years I obeyed my depressive emotions and started out badly. I did what I felt and only what I felt. I thought with my feelings and acted on my moods. Because I studied when I felt like it, instead of when I really needed to, my grades suffered. As a result, in the first two years I achieved very little. Because I followed my feelings instead of what was right and righteous, I fell into several destructive relationships that led to moral compromise and caused a lot of damage, both to me and to others. This led to still more depression and hopelessness. How did God respond? He sent me the finest woman I've ever known and made certain I married her. God is love, and that is more than just a theology.

All these years later I still experience discouragement. Once in a while I struggle with a season of depression. Usually that's when the people of my congregation have been less than wonderful in some way. But it always passes, and while it lasts, I refrain from self-condemnation. In short, seasons still come when negative feelings try to determine what I see and choose in life. There's nothing wrong with that. No feeling is a "wrong" feeling. No one will ever again convince me that I have the wrong feelings or that God can't bless me because of them.

Faith isn't in the feelings except as my heart learns by experience to truly know and trust God so that real joy and peace take hold. It takes a lot less energy to rest in God's goodness than it does to struggle with fear, uncertainty, and depression. Meanwhile, no matter what I'm feeling, I strive to choose to do the right thing in obedience, even putting myself in positions where, unless God provides, I will most likely fail.

For instance, the numbers never work, but I tithe anyway. I always have and I always will. God has never failed to meet me there and cover every need, even when I've been less than wise with my finances. As I said earlier, I planted my current congregation from nothing, with no support from any organization or even any outside authority to bless it. I did it in fear and I did it not wanting to do it, but I did it because it was the right thing to do in obedience to God. Over the years God has consistently met me and paid every bill. Less than two months into that church-plant, I was on full-time salary. We were multi-staffed less than two months after that!

Faith is in the doing, in the obedient act. It neither begins nor ends as an emotion, although the satisfaction and joy it brings can be tremendous. Too many of us are waiting to have a feeling before we do what we've been called to do or what we know we should do to move forward in life. We think faith is a feeling that we must have (or, at least some of it) before we can do things that involve risk. Believing that the feeling makes things possible, we get religious about it, striving in the flesh to get enough of the feeling to believe we have the faith. Then, because the feeling never happens, we fail to take the act of faith that puts us in position to receive what God has reserved for us. The result? Disappointment.

What if Abraham had never left Ur? God would have loved him and provided for him anyway. But destiny—fathering a nation and a company of nations through which God poured out the revelation of Himself—would never have happened. God wanted sons of Abraham, not sons of Terah. Canaan was the Promised Land, not Ur.

You might be thinking the feeling will make it easy, that if you have the feeling then the feeling is faith, and faith like that will pave your way with flowers. If so, that's why you've been stuck. Jesus accomplished the cross as an incredibly difficult act of faith done in obedience, not done as something He felt He wanted to do. I doubt the apostle Paul felt much like preaching on those occasions when he knew it would get him whipped, beaten, and maybe killed. These things were costly acts of obedience that constituted faith, not some mysterious, positive inner feeling or emotion—and look at the outcome!

Will it ever be easy? Probably not. For this reason the author of Hebrews wrote that it is for discipline that you "endure" (Heb. 12:7). Through discipline we grow up into the peaceful fruit of righteousness as we overcome difficulty.

My wife and I left for seminary in Pasadena, California, from northern Idaho in 1973 with just enough money to get us there and no idea how we would support ourselves when we arrived. A month earlier we didn't even know how we'd pay for tuition, until God provided the necessary scholarship, granted by a charitable foundation weeks after I had been told there were no more scholarships available.

As I piloted the U-Haul truck down the freeway, a $300 car in tow and my newly pregnant wife next to me dry-heaving with morning sickness, I could feel only cold apprehension and fear. Three years of graduate school lay before me, and I was scared spitless. We had no money at all, and we were moving far from any of our family to spend three years in a strange city we had never seen. We hadn't even secured housing. Most people would say that we were out of our minds, but the move was an act of faith in the absence of emotional certainty. God didn't look down from heaven on us and mutter, "Well, you just didn't feel enough faith, so I'm doing nothing for you." He provided because that's who He is and because we obeyed.

Was it easy? Decidedly not. I labored twenty hours

a week as a youth pastor in a local church, in addition to carrying what the seminary told us would require fifty-five hours a week for the full course of study. On top of that, I painted apartments and did the gardening in our apartment complex to raise the money to feed my family. I sought out old furniture, refinished it, and sold it in the classifieds. I did all this while carrying a maximum academic load. It was difficult, to say the least, and it tested my strength at every level, but God met us there. Faith seldom makes anything easy, but it does make things possible.

A FINAL LOOK

Faith doesn't originate with us and our capacity to feel some kind of certainty. It consists of understanding and trusting who God really is and what He's truly like. Consider one final look at the truth that what you feel in your heart has little or nothing to do with how God treats you, and that real faith lies in the act of obedience, not emotion. It's demonstrated in Matthew 8.

"And behold, there arose a great storm on the sea, so that the boat was being covered with the waves; but Jesus Himself was asleep. And they came to Him and woke Him, saying, 'Save us, Lord; we are perishing!'" (Matt. 8:24–25). Haven't there been times when you thought God had gone AWOL? These men had been spending 100 percent of their time following after Jesus, witnessing His works, and soaking in the revelation of the Father in Jesus; and still they fell into fear and unbelief.

"He said to them, 'Why are you afraid, you men of *little faith*?' Then He got up and rebuked the winds and the sea, and it became perfectly calm" (v. 26, emphasis added). Jesus woke up rubbing His eyes, apparently completely untroubled at the danger they all faced, and calmly ordered the storm to cease. Ultimately faith becomes a relationship of trust based on a complete revelation of the nature of our God, not an emotional achievement or a means of coercing Him into action on our behalf. The disciples needed to come to know who Jesus really was. As the perfect revelation of the Father's unfathomable love, He didn't decide to let them drown over their fear and lack of trust.

Faith is seldom about what God will or will not do. Despite His disciples' *lack* of faith, Jesus stilled the storm and saved them, but they could have been spared the stress and fear. Jesus longs to bring us to the place of rest and peace. At rest with the Father, He slept through the storm while the disciples panicked. And though He seemed a bit irritated at their lack of trust, Jesus wasn't put off by the disciples' unbelieving panic. The *act* of faith on their part, in the absence of real trust, was to cry out to Jesus in their fear. My personal emotional unbelief has never kept God from acting on my behalf. Rather, it kept me in turmoil and fear until Jesus in love did what He was going to do anyway.

The substance of real faith is a revelation of the true nature and love of the Father, not some ill-defined quantity of emotional certainty generated by human effort. Yes, Jesus said more than once in various ways, "Your faith has made you well," but in each instance the substance of that faith began with the recognition of who Jesus was and what He was like.

In each case the faith that resulted from the revelation

of the nature of our Lord found expression in an action. The woman with the flow of blood, for instance, pushed through a crowd to touch His garment (Mark 5:27–34). Of the men who tore a hole in the roof to let down the paralytic the Scripture says, "Seeing their faith" (Luke 5:18–20), but notice in this instance as well that the revelation of who Jesus was led to an action (probably one the owner of the house wasn't too pleased with!).

We have often been mistaken in having faith *that* God will do something, rather than having faith *in* who He is. The former can be manipulation. The latter is real relationship. I have long since stopped trying to have the right feelings and have set my will to know the heart of my Father through Jesus. Faith *in* Him roots me in the revelation of who He is. It frees me from the need to generate an emotion erroneously defined as faith *that* He will do something I wish Him to do.

Never again will I permit anyone to convince me that I have the wrong feelings or that God can't bless me because of them. On the other hand, if I can help it, I will never allow my feelings to keep me from obediently acting in faith in a way that puts me in position to receive the victory in life. It's not only my personal victory that's at stake. Also at stake are all the people who will be let down if I obey my feelings of doubt, fear, and uncertainty rather than heeding the word of the Lord. The same is true for you, no matter your station or position in the church or in life.

On the other hand, I know that if I fail to act in faith, God will yet provide for me because in His incredible love He's faithful when I'm not. If, however, I want to obtain the victory, rise to a destiny, and be true to the people God has called me to minister to, then I must choose to act in obedience.

If what I say is true, then you might be asking, "What is the value of all that positive confession?" Well, it's certainly not to manipulate God into doing something that I want Him to do. Manipulation will always be violation of relationship. Neither can I find anything in Scripture, taken in context, that tells me I can create anything in the real world by my words. That's God's prerogative, not mine. He is the Creator. I am the created.

Positive confession builds hope and trust into my own spirit, and therein lies the value. Proverbs 12:25, for instance, says, "Anxiety in a man's heart weighs it down, but a good word makes it glad." A similar verse is Proverbs 16:24: "Pleasant words are a honeycomb, sweet to the soul and healing to the bones."

I have couched this chapter in the personal terms and experience of my own journey to freedom, but I have done so knowing that the outcome of my experience describes where a great many of you live as well. Stop being imprisoned in a form of salvation by works in which you strive to generate a set of feelings you call "faith." Rather, choose to act in obedience, regardless of the condition of your heart, and to seek rest in a revelation of the true nature of the Father who loves you beyond your capacity to understand.

Striving will always bring the disappointment so many of us feel. Grace brings the revelation of who our wonderful Trinitarian God really is. Therein lies freedom and a depth of satisfaction that goes beyond words.

Chapter 4

TWO PILLARS OF A
FRUITFUL LIFE

———— ◦ ————

F or more than forty years the body of Christ has
been too influenced by self-serving teachings
that promised to chart a course to personal prosperity,
personal blessing, experience of the supernatural, and
healing for the pain our self-orientation inevitably creates. The teachings produced best-selling books, built
megachurches, and launched popular Christian TV
programs.

As this wave of self-focused material washed over
us, how many of us missed the central truth of the
gospel—that Jesus didn't die on the cross and rise again
to make us rich or grant us an easy life, but to trans-
form the nature of who and what we are for eternity. I
know for certain that He didn't make that sacrifice to
entertain us. He came, rather, to reveal the nature and
character of His Father. (See John 14:9.) He also came
to impart that same nature and character into us, first
by cleansing our sin and then by making us one with

Himself in both a death and a life like His. (See Galatians 2:20.)

If we're ready to, then let's openly admit that off-balance, self-serving doctrines haven't worked well for most of us. By anyone's measure, divorce rates are higher than they should be, and, in my long experience as a pastor, I have seen that too many marriages fall far short of the satisfaction and joy God intends for us. As they come of age, our children abandon both church and faith at the rate of something like 75 percent to 80 percent, never to return.[1]

Our happiness quotient rates distressingly low, even in renewal circles where we're supposed to know better. Obviously we have missed it somewhere. Out of the disappointment and pain created by our misfocus, a new movement, a new wave of the Spirit, has started to build.

If you're reading this book, you're probably among those who are responding to a call from heaven for a significant shift of focus. The call is gathering strength in the hearts of a great number of hungry believers. This new movement, this thrust of the Spirit, is not about receiving from God—although in His love He never stops giving, and we therefore will never stop receiving. God loves to give, and one way we bless His heart is by gratefully receiving what He sends. This new thing, however, focuses not on receiving from God but on what we're becoming in Him. It's about an impartation of the Father's heart, nature, and character into us through the crucifixion and resurrection of Jesus until we can truly be called sons and daughters of God—ones who, from the deepest reaches of our own hearts, radiate the nature and character of our Father.

"But as many as received Him, to them He gave the right to become children of God" (John 1:12). As I previously noted, in Hebrew linguistic usage, to be a "son of" or a "child of" something is to resemble that thing in a significant way. "For the anxious longing of the creation waits eagerly for the revealing of the sons of God" (Rom. 8:19). A time is coming—and in some ways now is—when God will openly reveal a generation of believers whose passion has been to absorb the nature and character of the God we serve.

The movement I speak of centers on the nature of the Father imparted into us in character, disposition, heart, and spirit. It moves us toward conformity to "the image of His Son" (Rom. 8:29) and into transformation of character from the inside out until we have the Father's heart as our own. Those of us who can hear the call are moving from "receiving" to 'becoming." This means the focus of life in the Holy Spirit has shifted from the remedial (repairing the damage we've done to ourselves) to the transformational (changing everything we are from the inside out). The Spirit of Jesus must take captive every thought, every emotion, and every inclination so the nature of the Father shines from us and through us.

With this transformation the world will see Him and know Him by what they see and sense in us. Never in my lifetime have I known a season when integrity and honor counted for more. We must now respond to the call of the Holy Spirit by placing a new emphasis on the cross and the blood of Jesus, pondering and studying these foundations of our faith until the selfless sacrifice He made for us becomes the heart of our own character.

When the cross and the blood become reality in us, we will see life and faith begin to work as God intended from the beginning.

This calls for rearranging priorities in our relationship with God. At some level most of us relate to God with a credo that goes something like this: "If God doesn't prosper me and I have trouble paying my bills, then does God really love me?"

Perhaps you think, "I'm fat and can't seem to get the weight off, and I feel terrible about myself. So how can God really favor me?" Or you might feel, "I've had all the stress I can take. Where are You, Lord? Are You really on my side?" Others cry out, "If I keep encountering stone walls in that job search, does God really favor me? Why is He blessing somebody else with a good job and not me?" If you're a Christian professional, as I am, you might think, "I'm a pastor. If God grows my church, then He loves me and favors me. But if He doesn't, then I'm depressed and wonder if He's there for me and whether I am really called to ministry." (Been there, done that!)

It seems that if everything goes well, then our excitement grows: "God loves me! God is blessing me!" When things aren't going so well, we tend to draw the opposite conclusion. You're thinking that if God really loved you, then He would do all the things for you that you really need Him to—or at least you wouldn't be struggling against the obstacles and difficulties you're facing.

In truth, He does love you, and He has given you the most important gift of all, if you'll receive it. Jesus's sacrifice made it possible for Him to grant you His own nature, His own righteousness, and His own goodness. You won't just wear it like a cloak that has been imparted to you while merely concealing the unbroken sin beneath. You will become it as you seek Him and embrace it. "He made Him who knew no sin to be sin on our behalf, so that we might become the righteousness of God in Him" (2 Cor. 5:21). Neither a theory nor a mere positional theology, this injection of real character changes everything. We are moving from a mind-set of passively receiving into a season of actively becoming who we are in Him.

If you remain fixated on receiving, then you'll always be disappointed with your faith and your experience with God. You'll be stuck in a fruitless focus on self. But when you refocus on becoming and being made over in His selfless image, yielding to His gentle hand, you will ultimately find no end of joy and satisfaction. As you grow in oneness with Him, you will see true life, love, and power result.

We are, however, engaged in a great culture war. Wars have always been about possession of territory and control of resident populations. In this war your heart, thoughts, life, and spirit are the territory your enemy, the devil, strives to occupy and influence, claiming it as His own.

The culture around us, inspired and dominated by a demonic principality of self-focus and personal prosperity, conditions us to base life on perceptions rooted in self and what self desires. If we allow it to do so, the culture blinds us to the essence of what we've really been given as believers. In that blindness we fall into disappointment when polluted and misfocused teachings that cater to self-focus fail to deliver on their promises. This often leads us to question our faith itself, which is what our enemy wanted all along.

This new move of the Spirit I see developing appeals to people who have grown tired of the broken promises, the hype, and the pretense of a faith that starts from the wrong foundation. It reaches people weary of noise, words, and teachings that don't work out the way the teachers claim. It speaks to a hunger for a deeper reality, a new realization of what our faith is truly all about.

Jesus does love us. He loves us so desperately that He gave His own life not just to forgive our sin—that's where many folks stop seeking—but also to clothe and fill us with His own righteousness, goodness, and love. It's the gift of His own nature, His ways imparted into us. God loves us enough to grant us the power to become something glorious in reflection of His own image.

If you became a believer in Jesus just so you could go to heaven, then you missed what it's really all about. God seeks to move us from a focus on what we can receive to what we can become in Him. What we can become is a wonderful gift of the Father's selfless and loving heart revealed and imparted in and through Jesus.

Foundational Pillars

The revelation of who God is

Moses knew the Lord like no one before him, and it came about because he asked the right questions. The two most foundational things Moses asked of God were "Who are You?" and "Show me Your ways." On these two pillars rested his entire life and ministry:

> Then Moses said to God, "Behold, I am going to
> the sons of Israel, and I will say to them, 'The
> God of your fathers has sent me to you.' Now they
> may say to me, 'What is His name?' What shall I
> say to them?" God said to Moses, "I AM WHO I
> AM"; and He said, "Thus you shall say to the sons
> of Israel, 'I AM has sent me to you.'"
> —EXODUS 3:13–14

Moses wanted to know, "Who are You? Tell me what You're like. I need a revelation." God answered, "I AM. I exist. Time doesn't bind Me. All of reality exists in and because of Me."

That single revelation formed the basis for everything Moses subsequently accomplished in finding his own intimacy with the Lord, receiving the commandments of God, and selflessly leading the people through the wilderness to a promised land. The same applies to you and me. Ask the right questions, and you get the right answers. Ask the wrong questions, and you may get no answers at all. Maybe we shouldn't be asking *why* all these things happen to us in life. Why do we encounter these troubles? Why does it seem so hard sometimes? Real life begins with the question "Who are You?" It begins with seeking the revelation of who our God really is. Start there, and all the other answers flow more easily.

The revelation of God's ways

Moses made another request, just as important as his first:

> Then Moses said to the LORD, "See, You say to
> me, 'Bring up this people!' But You Yourself have
> not let me know whom You will send with me.
> Moreover, You have said, 'I have known you by
> name, and you have also found favor in My sight.'
> Now therefore, I pray You, if I have found favor
> in Your sight, let me know Your ways that I may
> know You, so that I may find favor in Your sight."
> —EXODUS 33:12–13

He meant: "Yes, I know I have Your favor to perform
miracles and to force Pharaoh to let the people go and
to part the Red Sea. I know all that. But I long for Your
favor, so show me Your *ways*. Not Your miracles or Your
power. Your *ways*."

Moses knew that the favor of God in success, power,
victory over enemies, authority over people, and ability
to perform signs and wonders would be dangerous
gifts in the absence of the more important gift of God's
nature and character—His ways. Having received a revelation of God's ways, Moses led the people, not for the
sake of building a power base, but out of love for God
and concern for the welfare of the nation. He led humbly
from a broken heart. He could have allowed wounding
to overtake him, and he could have resigned in discouragement and walked away when persecution and criticism came at him. But he didn't. Despite it all, he stood
and served for the Lord's sake, the Lord's honor, and
the good of the people God had placed on his heart.

He asked to know God's ways. He had questions. How
does God think? How does He feel? When the people
fall away, how does God respond? What motivates

Him? What are His mental and emotional processes? What is God really like?

Consider how those questions compare with ones about our own personal ways. What currents flow through your own heart? How easily are you offended? What makes you angry, and how quickly can you go there? How do you feel about people? When someone hates you, how do you respond? When everything goes wrong and the pressure is on, what goes through your mind and heart? When opposition comes against you, how do you feel? What do you do? What is your life focus?

Moses wanted to know about God's internal workings—His ways—in response to all those kinds of things so that he could make God's nature and character a part of himself. In doing so, he could obtain yet more favor, deeper intimacy with God, solid integrity, and greater revelation. When you know God's ways, you know Him.

Nothing came easily for Moses. The people grumbled, rebelled, and threatened to kill him. Nevertheless, in all of it he could see that the favor of God rested on him. It didn't rest in his success, but in something else more important to him that enabled him to grow into the great man he became. He saw God's favor in what God was creating in him through the revealing of His ways.

God offered him favor. Interpret that as *anointing*— "the power to lead and perform signs and wonders." It meant God would clear the way before Moses and grant him authority over people as He poured supernatural strength and power through him. Moses understood, however, that anointing without character, without the nature of God, without God's ways to sustain it, becomes a dangerous thing. He knew something that we too need to know: the greater favor comes with understanding and living in God's ways at the level of what you've become inwardly through Him.

This includes how God thinks, how God sees, how God loves, how God responds to adversity and deals with offense, how God handles power, and how God sees people. He told Moses, "You've already found favor with Me," and Moses responded, "I want to be like You in my own nature so that I may find *more* favor and more anointing." It's as if Moses were saying, "I want to be trusted with more. Therefore, make me more like You so that I can bear it."

Moses made two crucial requests of God: "Who are You?" and "Show me Your ways." They formed the two pillars of a fruitful life that set the course of Moses's destiny and made him one who changed history for us all. "Who are You?" and "Show me Your ways": they still resonate today. Every one of us who has committed his or her life to Jesus has been called as a history maker, to be part of a fresh move of God's Spirit focused on the cross, the blood of Jesus, and conforming to the image of the Son. Beyond merely receiving the Father's love, we must become the embodiment of His nature in our own lives and thus make a difference in this world.

THE IDOLATRY OF THE ANOINTING

For a very long time now much of the body of Christ has been falling down and worshipping at the altar of the anointing, filling auditoriums to be touched by the anointed superstar. I feel, however, that we've often focused there at the expense of an emphasis on character. In fact, in some circles, we continue to discourage confrontation of sin in leadership, equating it with "touching the Lord's anointed"—as if the scriptural admonition not to do so in 1 Chronicles 16:21–22 actually prohibits confrontation of sin. Apparently the prophet Nathan didn't see it that way when he confronted David after his adultery with Bathsheba and his order for her husband to be murdered!

Entire segments of the body of Christ have camped on the anointing, the power, the miracles, the excitement, and the hype. In fact, in many places we have been absorbed in teaching masses of people to be supernatural and "imparting" spiritual gifts, while neglecting the more important issues of character. As neglect of a focus on the cross, the blood, and the character of Jesus has grown, the number of scandals, moral compromises, adulteries, and financial abuses has escalated. As a result, when the world looks to us for integrity and hope, it finds us sadly lacking.

However, where character is emphasized before anointing, these failures become relatively rare, while the anointing, cradled in righteous character, lasts and grows in power. Historically revivals that emphasized the cross and the blood of Jesus didn't suffer the level of scandal and moral compromise we see today. In those instances, rather, history records men and women of God whose integrity could not be questioned and whose impact resonates through the ages.

Why? Because the cross and the blood bring transformation. Jesus's righteousness is imprinted upon us. This changes the way we behave; it determines personal choices, revitalizes families, and makes peace where there was war because it focuses us first on a concern for the welfare of others before our own. God set the universe up to work on the principle of sacrifice, and it cannot bring forth glory in any other way.

By itself, anointing lacks the power to change the one who carries it. Its function is to enable an ordinary man or woman to do extraordinary things—but it ends there. Samson, for instance, carried an amazing anointing but suffered shipwreck of his life over foundational flaws in his character. The power for change lies in the cross and resurrection. Paul explained this in Galatians 2:20: "I have been crucified with Christ; and it is no longer I who live, but Christ lives in me; and the life which I now live in the flesh I live by faith in the Son of God, who loved me and gave Himself up for me."

Understand that the cross and the blood carry power for more than forgiveness of sin. If you stopped at forgiveness when you prayed to receive Jesus, you missed the real promise. They express God's essential character in the most powerful manner. Take them out of the picture, de-emphasize them in favor of motivational or warm and fuzzy messages designed to fill the seats, and all you have left is noise—and ultimately disappointment. Why? Because real changes at the level of the heart just won't happen. As evidence, witness the sad moral state of the contemporary church!

Joy lies on the path of self-sacrifice! Jesus told His disciples, "If anyone wishes to come after Me, he must deny himself, and take up his cross and follow Me" (Matt. 16:24). In Mark 8:35 Jesus promises, "For whoever wishes to save his life will lose it, but whoever loses his life for My sake and the gospel's will save it."

My son, who serves as my co-pastor, once stated, "Dad, we're not called to put butts in seats and grow a church. We're called to make disciples." Jesus spoke to that same issue when He said, "Whoever does not carry his own cross and come after Me cannot be My disciple" (Luke 14:27), and when He issued His last earthly command: "Go therefore and make disciples of all the nations" (Matt. 28:19).

Has the modern church lost its central focus and thus its power? Isn't there an enormous difference between getting someone to say the sinner's prayer and making a disciple? "Take up your cross and follow Me" was an invitation to take on the character of Jesus. It invited the old self-centered nature that leads only to failure and depression to die to make way for something new and wonderful.

When anointing comes before character, disasters happen. King Saul, Israel's first king, never dealt with his character flaws. Roots of insecurity overcame him and destroyed his reign, his posterity, and eventually even his sanity. When the anointing fell on him, he won great victories for Israel, but in the end foundational character flaws destroyed him. He died a broken man after a defeat in battle.

Judas Iscariot carried the same anointing Jesus bestowed on the eleven other disciples when He sent them out on missionary journeys to heal the sick, cast out demons, and preach the kingdom. But like Saul, Judas never faced his character flaws. At the last, those gaping holes in his character destroyed him. After betraying Jesus to death, he ended his life with suicide. He could have known glory, but his name will instead be forever remembered in infamy.

When character change takes priority over favor and anointing, however, revolutions begin that shape and mold entire peoples and nations. This describes King David, Israel's second king. Far from perfect, he committed grievous sins, up to and including adultery and murder, but he was a man who faced his failings, owned the damage he did to others, and repented. I believe Psalm 139 came as a cry from the depth of his heart. I particularly love verses 23 and 24: "Search me, O God, and know my heart; try me and know my anxious thoughts; and see if there be any hurtful way in me, and lead me in the everlasting way." David became a world changer and died as the man after God's own heart. Through David's line came Jesus.

This is where we're going—those of us who find ourselves on this journey toward something more. Here lies the seedbed of a new move of God springing out of the hunger growing in the hearts of so many who long for the promise of something real.

"Who are You?" brings the revelation of the real nature of God the Father, God the Son, and God the Holy Spirit. "Show me Your ways!" opens the door to foundational transformation.

Chapter 5

YOU ARE THE LIGHT
OF THE WORLD

———•———

Disappointment often stems from failure to realize who and what we really are in the Lord. Failing to comprehend this leads in turn to loss of a sense of purpose. Closely related to hope, purpose gives us a reason for pressing forward in life. How many of us would go to work every day if there were no hope of receiving a paycheck? What would be the purpose?

Self-focus can never provide a sense of purpose or fulfillment sufficient to sustain a life. Yet, conditioned by the surrounding culture, this is where huge numbers of us have been stuck without realizing it. We have been called to the life of the cross in oneness with Jesus. Nothing less than life given away for the sake of others and the glory of Jesus will ever be enough—but that doesn't mean that our lives just disappear. Jesus didn't give His life to erase ours. He gave it to restore us to the Father's original plan. In Him we come to understand who and what we truly are.

In the ancient Middle East the homes of ordinary people were usually constructed of mud bricks and had no windows. Even in the daytime the interior of such a home would be dark because the only light came from the doorway. For the average family the house consisted of one room with a dirt floor and a raised area on which to sleep. A single oil lamp placed on a stand gave light to the whole house. Jesus therefore likened the world around us to a darkened house in which stands a solitary lamp to light it up. We are that lamp. He means for us to be seen:

> You are the light of the world. A city set on a hill cannot be hidden; nor does anyone light a lamp and put it under a basket, but on the lampstand, and it gives light to all who are in the house. Let your light shine before men in such a way that they may see your good works, and glorify your Father who is in heaven.
> —MATTHEW 5:14-16

In John 8:12 Jesus said about Himself, "I am the Light of the world"—and He is certainly that—but in Matthew 15:14 He said something very different: "*You* are the light of the world" (emphasis added). We Christians tend to repeat a number of religious statements we've been taught over the years, accepting them without much question, unaware of their inaccuracy and the harm they do. On the surface they sound great, and we receive them because they seem so good and holy.

For instance, when someone expresses admiration for us, we say: "Don't look at me. Look at Jesus"; or when complimented, we protest: "It wasn't me. It was Jesus."

With either instance we unwittingly dishonor the one who gave the compliment and deprive him or her of the joy of having given it. In the process we place a cloud or a basket over the light that Jesus says we are.

When saying these things, we think we're honoring Him, but in reality we're minimizing the glory of what He's done in us and obscuring the glory He created when He saved and filled us. We want to be humble, but we don't really understand what that means. We therefore say these things for the wrong reasons, failing to truly believe what Jesus Himself has declared about us. Glorifying Jesus can never mean erasing you. Jesus can only be fully glorified when we fully own the identity and destiny He won for us through the cross and resurrection. Fail to recognize this, and you will forever carry a heaviness that sucks the life and joy from your walk with Him.

We mean well when we say, "I want to be invisible so that Jesus can shine." But we're making a statement at odds with what Jesus actually taught. Jesus meant something more like, "I want *you* to be *very* visible so that I can shine in and through the wonder of what you've become in Me." The world can't see Jesus. They see you and me. And it's you and me the Lord uses. He longs to exalt us and reveal us to the world so that the nations can admire His handiwork in us and therefore witness how great He is. The apostle Paul wrote: "For God, who said, 'Light shall shine out of darkness,' is the One who has shone in our hearts to give the Light of the knowledge of the glory of God in the face of Christ" (2 Cor. 4:6).

Never has He desired to erase us, hide us, or conceal

us. What real father would want that for his children? My own three children and nine grandchildren are the pride of my life. Showing them off is my joy. Our heavenly Father has only ever wished to exalt us, to show us off to the world. That's the depth of His love. It's possible for us to adopt such inappropriate self-deprecating statements because we don't really believe what Jesus says about us and because we have failed to understand the Father's heart for us.

RISING HIGHER

I know a young woman who married a man from a culture in which it is considered dishonorable for a son to rise higher than the level of his father. As a result, that entire culture struggles with poverty and oppression. We in the body of Christ have too often cultivated a Christian culture that in some ways practices this same crippling philosophy in our relationship with God.

Every true father wants his son or daughter to rise higher than himself, and when that happens, he wants the world to see it and know it. In the same way, our Father in heaven, who loves us perfectly, desires for us to rise higher. When we do this, He wants to show us off to the world. Jesus said, "Let your light shine before men," and then they'll know how great God is.

This explains His statement in John 14:12, "Truly, truly, I say to you, he who believes in Me, the works that I do, he will do also; and greater works than these he will do; because I go to the Father." He could have said, "I'll do those greater works through you," but asserted instead, "You'll do them." We'll do those greater things because Jesus goes to the Father, whose heart is to exalt His children as His children exalt Him. He dreamed of the day when we would do greater things on this earth than He did in His own earthly walk. We are the light of the world. We're not supposed to be invisible.

Some of us have been taught that the flow of the Holy Spirit through us is like water flowing through a pipe, unaffected by the pipe, but this misrepresents the dynamic. You're involved. It's not just Jesus who is involved, but rather you *with* Him.

For instance, Isaiah spoke for God, but he spoke in a way unique to him. His nature and character flavored the expression even as the purity of the prophetic word flowed through him. Matthew, Mark, Luke, and John told the same story in the New Testament, but each one expressed the same inspiration differently as it passed through the filter of their individual personalities and perceptions. As friends of Christ, you and I are co-laborers with God, as 1 Corinthians 3:9 says: "For we are God's fellow workers." You're doing the works too. You're involved, and He's doing it with you!

The idea that we must be invisible, that we don't count, or that every good thing we do is just Him and only Him is a lie from the pit of the religious spirit designed to undo what Jesus accomplished for us through the cross and resurrection. It negates what He did when He forgave us, filled us with His Spirit, made us whole, and declared us to be holy. It dishonors the glory of the uniqueness of His creation in each of us.

A Light in the Darkness

As we continue to witness the catastrophic collapse of a once great Western society, darkness will deepen. Most us know and understand that light shines brightest in darkness. Anyone who has tried to read the lighted screen on his iPad in the bright sunlight and failed, but was then blinded by that same screen after opening it upon awakening in a darkened room, understands what I mean. The darker the world around us, the brighter we shine in the midst of it.

Is what I'm saying about the collapse of Western culture true? In the 1950s divorce hovered around 2 percent.[2] The most casual observer knows that this number has risen significantly. I'm overwhelmed at how many children in this culture live in homes in which, if there's a man in the house at all, he's not the birth father. My own father pastored before me. In the 1950s he kept the church sanctuary open twenty-four hours a day. Even thieves respected God's house and left it alone. A generation later, I carry a heavy set of keys because we find we need different locks for every section of our church. Even so-called Christians will steal from us. My father left the keys in his car every day, and we never experienced a theft. Because we didn't need to, we never locked our house. I never saw a key. Today almost one in one hundred Americans is in prison. We have the largest prison population in the world, as a percentage of the population.[2] Security systems for homes have become a major industry.

Sexually transmitted diseases have become a widespread plague because our sense of morality is gone. My father once wisely stated that it has never been the case that venereal disease was contracted between a man and a woman whose only sexual activity was with each other! We've not only cast God's laws aside, but we've also grown blind to the reasons the rules exist in the first place.

Generally people are miserable. Antidepressants have become one of the most prescribed drugs in the Western world,[3] and suicide is the third-leading cause of death among the younger generation[4] because they have no hope, no God, and no sense of destiny or purpose.

It's a darkening world, and we are the light within it, together with our brothers and sisters in faith. God has called us as a lighthouse people in the gathering darkness. "Let your light shine before men in such a way that they may see your good works, and glorify your Father who is in heaven" (Matt. 5:16).

Jesus stated the purpose for not obscuring the light, "That they may see your good works." How do we define the *good works*? Aren't you tired of listening to all those voices pronouncing condemnation on sinners and calling it *light*? Or working so hard to please God and always seeming to fall short?

I suggest that much of the disappointment so many of us feel with church—and Christianity in general— stems from the same lack of understanding of the Father's heart that infected the Pharisees. Handing down condemnation based on the Law or striving to earn some righteousness so that God will notice us can make us feel so powerful and important. Yet the heart of the Father, as revealed in Jesus, is to take us lower in order to serve and lift even the worst of those who are lost:

> For God so loved the world, that He gave His only begotten Son, that whoever believes in Him shall not perish, but have eternal life. For God did not send the Son into the world to judge the world, but that the world might be saved through Him.
> —John 3:16–17

The Works in People

The "works" Jesus referred to can be seen in the young woman who came to us a number of years ago as a methamphetamine addict. The state had taken her children, and she had lost every shred of hope. Today she has been clean of substance abuse for a number of years, her children have been restored to her, and she has been earning a college degree. The presence of God radiates from her. The Father's heart through Jesus did that as believers let their light shine in love upon her. The world can see the light emanating from a life like that, and it can only be attributed to our Father. This redeemed and restored woman didn't have to perform for God or white-knuckle her recovery. As we who are the light of the world obediently gave the love God showed us, she received it from a Father who loves her.

Let it shine! There's hope in the world!

A teenager came to us as an abuser of his siblings, a high school dropout known by every detention center in town, and a drug user stoned on something every day. Today he's a leader, he's proclaiming the gospel and leading others to Jesus, and he's earning a college degree all because believers let their light shine in such a way that it melted his heart. Condemnation couldn't do that. It never will be able to.

Our light shines in the joy and security you see in the children of a solid home where the parents know the Lord, as opposed to the confusion and chaos in the world around them. Something shining from that family makes a statement to a dying world and gives hope to those who've lost it.

The culture around us has shifted from covenant, commitment, and sacrifice for the sake of others to a focus on self that says if you don't make me happy, then I'm taking a hike. Misery, loneliness, and hurt remain. By contrast, when our marriages stand out healthy and strong, it's a "work" that shines before the world and makes a declaration of the glory of our God.

My wife and I have been married forty-one years, since 1972 at this writing, and people look at us and say, "You give us hope." People whose lives have been a train wreck come to me personally to express what an inspiration my marriage and my family are to them. They say, "How did you do that?" That is the lamp in the dark place. It is an example of the good works Jesus spoke of, not performed legalistically, but simply lived out in the wholeness Jesus has given for all to see.

THE WORKS IN SERVICE, SIGNS, AND WONDERS

The church I pastor feeds hundreds of homeless people each week, operates a food bank that keeps dozens of families nourished, and provides a counseling ministry free of charge to the community. We reach out to Native American reservations, not only to train and support Native American pastors we've ordained but also to deliver huge amounts of material support. We are not a megachurch at the time of this writing. We simply choose to risk ourselves to let our light shine so that our good works bring glory to our Lord and Father.

Signs and wonders follow. Over the years we've seen God fill teeth with gold, heal diabetes, restore bad backs, heal damaged hearts, perform miracles of multiplication, and more. These things follow where the kingdom of God is realized.

I focus here, however, on the works that require real, tangible sacrifice in love. Sometimes the miraculous can be too easy, asking little of us. If we want our works to shine in a way that impresses and wins the world, we're going to have to make real sacrifices in material ways and couple that with the touch of the supernatural.

Light stands out in darkness. Let that light shine. God wants you to be seen. He wants to show you off for the glory of what He has done in you. All you have to do is be yourself, expressing outwardly what He has created inwardly. Know who you are. The Spirit of God glows in you. Let people caught in the darkness of the culture around you be attracted not as much by what you preach (your ideas and doctrines) as by who and what you have become, showing that in your deeds.

"You are the light of the world"—stand out, and make no apology for it!

THE POWER OF ONE LIGHT

On a missions trip to Eastern Europe we ministered in a city in south central Ukraine. This being a major metro area of about a million people, the church there appointed us a driver to chauffeur us around. Thus we met a former Soviet army colonel I'll call Sergei, with the intimidating appearance of the army officer he once was. Beneath his tough exterior, however, lay a gentle heart of gold.

Sergei eagerly told us his story, and I never tire of repeating it.

In his army unit was a young private, a Baptist Christian. Each day the men lined up in formation to recite the pledge of allegiance to the USSR. On the basis of his Christian conscience, this young private refused. Obviously this caused a problem for Sergei, who perceived it as a threat to discipline in the ranks. Frustrated and having no idea what to do, he decided to speak with the young private's pastor, and together they worked out a solution. The private could recite the pledge up to the part that violated his conscience, at which point he could remain silent; because everyone else would be facing forward at attention, no one would notice.

So far so good, except that Sergei now considered this young man to be a troublemaker. To deal with the issue, he began to assign this Baptist conscript all the worst jobs, from cleaning toilets to shoveling mud. It wasn't long, though, before he noticed something he didn't expect. No matter what he did to this young man, he never heard a complaint out of him, never a hint of rebellion or anger. He saw only the heart of an obedient servant. Looking a bit deeper, he saw that when the other members of his unit had problems, they turned to this Baptist private for counsel and solace. Sergei told us, "That was the first drop in the bucket toward me repenting and becoming a Christian."

As so often happens when cultures deny God, crime and theft run rampant—and so it did in the culture of the Soviet army. Twice or more every year each commander had to go before the "minister," as they called the government representative, to account for conditions under his command. No commander ever looked forward to these meetings. A Christian at this point, Sergei sought the counsel of his pastor about how to reduce the crime rate in his unit in advance of his next meeting with the Soviet minister.

"Well, do you pray for your men?" the pastor queried. Sergei took his pastor's advice and began to pray. At the next meeting with the government minister he reported that crime in his unit had decreased to nearly nothing. In fact, he made up two incidents that didn't really happen, hoping to stave off an accusation that he was lying about the crime rate.

The minister accused him of lying anyway, insisting that such a huge reduction in crime could not have happened. An investigation was launched in which it was found that Sergei had lied about the two incidents to prevent being accused of lying about the reduction in crime. After admonishing him never to lie again, the minister clearly stated that the reduction in crime had to be because of God; otherwise it would have been impossible.

Sergei's wife then became a believer through her

husband. She served as an aide to the commander of another unit. She too sought her pastor's counsel about what she could do as a believer and began to pray. This led to the conversion of her unit's political officer. In the USSR a political officer was, in effect, the priest of the Communist way, charged with enforcing proper Communist doctrine and holding the military rank of major. Speaking to such a person about Jesus therefore involved tremendous risk, as atheism was historically the official Communist Party doctrine with regard to religion. She obeyed God, however, not allowing the light to be obscured by fear. Hearing the truth in her heart and her words, the major gave his life to Jesus.

Struggling now with how to continue spouting Communist doctrine in conflict with his newfound faith, the political officer also sought out his pastor for advice, asking, "What do I do now?" His pastor told him that he must tell his troops about God. The next Sunday the major ordered the entire unit to church, marching them in formation to the building. They filled the back of the hall and listened to the sermon. Afterward, as the pastor issued the altar call, the major ordered the troops to march to the front and receive Jesus. They obeyed.

All this came about because one insignificant, no-name private in the army of a godless government refused to allow a basket to be placed over his light. Darkness gathered around him, but light shines brightest in dark places. His simple witness and servant's heart were the pebble that started a landslide. He could have protested and complained of injustice, but he chose to be a servant, strategically placed, who acted in love and bore enormous fruit.

HIDING THE LIGHT

Jesus commanded us not to hide or conceal the light He says that we are. What hides the light? What's the bushel that comes over our lamps? It can be fear of persecution or penalty, but most often it's the barrier of self-definition. *A self-definition at odds with the one God holds for you, that is at odds with the way He sees you, creates a cloud around you.* That cloud of negative self-definition obscures the light flowing out from the Holy Spirit who has filled you.

Outsiders see and sense this cloud. When that happens, and they find out that you're a Christian, then instead of seeing and feeling a light that appeals to them, calls to them, and lights up their lives, they perceive only that you have a set of ideas. Ideas aren't enough. With that cloud obscuring your light, they cannot see you as being any different from them. Faulty identity and self-definition, programmed in by parents, teachers, siblings, and peers, form the basis for this obscuring cloud. Composed of hurtful things that have been said to us and done to us, or that people failed to say and do, it amounts to forms of love not given.

In the movie *Pay It Forward* a single mother recovering from alcohol addiction is raising her little boy when her abusive, alcoholic, former husband returns. She listens to his promises, believes him, and allows him back into the home, giving him one more chance. This interrupts the budding relationship she has with her son's teacher—a good man who has recently come into her life. The teacher, having grown up with an abusive stepfather who actually set him on fire with gasoline, sees the abuse coming from the ex-husband and, worried for the little boy, begins to confront the mother about it.

Obviously failing to hear his warnings, she protests that her ex-husband has changed and won't hurt the boy, until the teacher finally explodes. "He doesn't have to hurt him!" he says. "All he has to do is not love him!" In the absence of love, the damage is done. Self-definition has been set in any one of its many harmful forms: not lovable, not chosen, not valued, ungifted, unattractive, unintelligent, loser, weak, poor.

Jesus, however, says that we are sons and daughters of our Father in heaven. Among many other passages of Scripture Paul wrote, "Blessed be the God and Father of our Lord Jesus Christ, who has blessed us with every spiritual blessing in the heavenly places in Christ...He predestined us to adoption as sons through Jesus Christ to Himself" (Eph. 1:3–5). The promise continues in verses 13–14: "In Him, you also, after listening to the message of truth, the gospel of your salvation—having also believed, you were sealed in Him with the Holy Spirit of promise, who is given as a pledge of our inheritance." Because we are His children, we inherit from Him. He gives the Holy Spirit as a pledge, a piece of the whole granted as a guarantee of the fullness to come.

Ephesians 2 drives home the position we now occupy:

> But God, being rich in mercy, because of His
> great love with which He loved us, even when we

were dead in our transgressions, made us alive together with Christ (by grace you have been saved), and raised us up with Him, and seated us with Him in the heavenly places in Christ Jesus.
—EPHESIANS 2:4–6

The right hand where Jesus sits is the place of authority and honor. In some way that no one this side of heaven can fully understand, we have already been seated with Jesus in the place of honor and authority.

Finally, in very different words, Ephesians 2:10 affirms what Jesus declared concerning our identity as light in this world. "For we are His workmanship, created in Christ Jesus for good works, which God prepared beforehand so that we would walk in them"—an affirmation not so different in content and meaning from Matthew 5:16: "Let your light shine before men in such a way that they may see your good works, and glorify your Father who is in heaven."

Those who fail to recognize who they really are will never walk in that identity. The result will be a measure of the disappointment and frustration many of us feel. We have been adopted as sons and daughters, chosen and transformed. Our Father is a king. We have an inheritance. As the light of the world, we have been destined to do greater works than Jesus, but we need to take the cover off the light and send the cloud away.

A PERSONAL STRUGGLE

For many years I struggled with an identity as one who was stolen from, steeped in rejection, never picked for the team, and mocked for being a preacher's kid. I was therefore never able to gather in or reap in proportion to the effort I poured out in life and ministry. I saw myself as the poor kid who never had anything. There's the cloud!

If I allow that cloud to remain, the light radiating from me will dim in proportion to my disagreement with God about who I am. I will have covered it with a bushel. Romans 12:2 says, "And do not be conformed to this world, but be transformed by the renewing of your mind, so that you may prove what the will of God is, that which is good and acceptable and perfect." Isn't that a lot like, "You are the light of the world," proving and demonstrating that God's will is good, acceptable, and perfect? When my mind and heart agree with His mind and heart—beginning with who I am—then I'm free to prove that God is good, unobscured, and unhindered.

The question is whether you and I will live according to what a dark world full of sinners has told us about ourselves or according to what Jesus won for us on the cross, through His resurrection, and in giving us the gift of His Spirit. You can go to counseling from now until the turn of the next century to get at the roots of your issues, to talk about them, and to get prayer. But until you decide to think of yourself as God thinks of you, to own your inheritance, and live like royalty with authority, freedom, a sense of privilege, chosenness, and favor, you will remain imprisoned. Take the bushel off the light, and gain the victory over that nagging sense of disappointment!

A PERSONAL COMMITMENT

Each of us is destined for great things. Why? Because we have a king for a Father who is best glorified when His children rise to be seen as His workmanship. I've made a personal determination that I will not live my life at a lesser level of destiny than God intended for me. I refuse to live wrapped in the cloud and thus cheat the people I love—and the people I will love in the future— out of the glory that is my birthright to dispense. I have determined not to live the rest of my life under a cloud of lies, and, to the extent I can influence others, I will not allow them to do so either. I will bring my thinking, my mind, and my attitude about myself into alignment with the Word of God. I commit to be intolerant of any thought or attitude in myself that fails to line up with God's view of me, and I therefore choose to live and believe in the way He sees me.

Righteous beliefs and attitudes almost never happen by accident. They don't grow from moods or feelings or result from some outside stimulus. These things are the fruit of decisions made with determination and per- severance by hungry and desperate people who have decided to live as God designed them to live in the power of the Holy Spirit. I choose to be that kind of man, and I will take others with me.

Ultimately we change not for our own sake, but because we've become desperate for others. This begins with family, friends, and other believers. Finally it touches the world. The hungry ones for whom I write bear a heart that cries, "I want to know that I lived for something, that when I go to heaven, I can say, 'I did it! I did it all! And it was fun!'"

You *are* the light of the world. Nothing can change that. All you need to do is take the cover off the light. Many of us have been wrapped in the darkness of a faulty self-definition all our lives—and I'm not talking about just poor or troubled people. I'm also referring to business owners, managers, nurses, doctors, attorneys, financial planners, and others like them who have achieved something in life but have nevertheless not truly owned the identity given to us all in Jesus.

This faulty self-definition does not have the power to make you less than Jesus declares you to be. You are the light of the world. This isn't something you become but is rather an accomplished fact in Jesus. A lamp under a basket is still a lamp. But, like a basket placed over the lamp, a faulty self-definition can cover your light. This is why Jesus commands us not to cover it but to let it shine. You are what you are. You might as well agree with Him about it.

Begin to seek out every thought, every feeling, and every attitude that fails to line up with what it means to be adopted through the blood of Jesus as a son or daughter of the king of the universe. In a healthy, non-condemning way, become intolerant of those thoughts. Make war on them and tell yourself, "I am *not* going to live that way!" Do this, and you will become a cultural anomaly, a glorious misfit. The goodness radiating unhindered from you will light up the world around you.

It won't be just your ideas or words that touch people. It will be the power and love of the living God. People will see and feel something good and wholesome, something so in contrast with the world that they'll be mystified by it and will feel compelled to ask you where it comes from. They'll feed on your health, your relationships, your marriage, your joy, your peace, the stability of your children, and they'll be made healthier themselves just by being exposed to the power and love of God.

Take the cover off the light. Come into agreement with what God says about you. He's right. You're wrong. Give it up.

Chapter 6

SLAVERY, SONSHIP, AND BECOMING GOD'S FRIEND

————•————

W hen we look at the differences between slavery (the way God views it), sonship, and friendship, we see the reason that Jesus longs to call us "friends"—and why we tend to miss the incredible importance of this altogether:

> You are My friends if you do what I command you. No longer do I call you slaves, for the slave does not know what his master is doing; but I have called you friends, for all things that I have heard from My Father I have made known to you.
> —John 15:14–15

As a slave, I must obey my master's commands. I have no right to ask for an explanation and am granted no privilege of insight into the plans or the heart of my master. His commands and precepts must be followed to the letter without question and with no expectation of intimacy. This is the heart of religion. It articulates the rules but fails to plumb the depths of the heart that made the rules. Therein we see the religion many of us have been exposed to. We were told it would give us life, but in its lovelessness it has brought only disappointment.

Sonship is better, but doesn't really go far enough. As a child, I might love my natural father and live on the receiving end of his love for me. In that sense the child/parent relationship is mutual. The father loves his children, and the children enjoy his blessing and protection. But if the relationship stops there, the father may never take his children into his confidence as adults. Something precious will be lost.

With a friendship, however, comes intimacy and trust, a sharing of deep secrets and intentions of the heart. Jesus wants to call us "friends" just as He did the Twelve. The emptiness so many of us have felt can be filled only within the intimacy of friendship with God and all that the word *friend* implies. Slavery, no matter how well intentioned, can never satisfy the emptiness, nor can even the wonder of becoming sons and daughters. Being a son or daughter, wonderful as it is, just doesn't go far enough.

In the natural, my son will always be my son, and I will love him as such as long as I'm alive. If we stopped there, however, we would fall short of a greater glory and a deeper love. In the natural, my son has become my friend and my partner in ministry and has grown to be more than a son to me. Few of us, however, have ever experienced such a shift into friendship with God. It's time we did!

It's About Trust

Becoming God's friend involves both fulfillment of a condition and a reward. The condition is obedience to the commands of Jesus, but not in the legalistic sense. His "new commandment," that we should love one another (John 13:34), points to the heart of it, but this love cannot be performed by any effort of the flesh. It grows and thrives only in the obedience of changed character—in our heart and our nature conformed to His. Obedience then transitions from striving to perform and into an effortless expression of what I've become as I embrace the cross in oneness with Him. Such a change of character opens the way to revelation concerning the deep and intimate purposes of God, which are steeped in love, and therein lies the reward.

Too many of us, however, would receive Jesus's word about obedience through a religious filter that leads us to misinterpret His intent. We'd make it an issue of fleshly performance in obedience to a set of rules in order to earn something, just as the Pharisees did—a form of obedience that promises love but fails to deliver. And nothing could be further from the Savior's heart.

Jesus did not mean that you become His friend if you perform rightly, dance to His tune, work hard enough, and thus earn your place with Him. He didn't mean us to think or feel, "If I do enough, then He might accept me. If I'm perfect enough, I might earn my place. But if I stumble, He might throw me away. If I fail or fall short of obedience, then I won't have intimacy with Him." Too many of us hear His words in that spirit and consequently miss the point. Performance was never the issue; rather, character formation and the condition of the heart. It's what Scripture calls "the peaceful fruit of righteousness" (Heb. 12:11), formed under discipline but established in rest.

Real love is an unconditional gift, but friendship rests on trust. God searches for those He can trust. In my own life I love many people who interface with me in various ways, but I trust only a very few. I trust those who I am certain have a true heart for me and who value and love the same things I do. I might love and forgive a neighbor who trashes my yard and violates my privacy. That love will be unconditional, but he will never be a friend in whom I choose to confide. I trust those who I know will care for things that belong to me as if my things were their own. I trust them because they have my best interests at heart.

Friends of God therefore love what Jesus loves. We become His friends when we do what He commands us, and His command to us is to "love one another" (John 15:17). He meant: "If you obey My command to love one another, then I know you have My best interests at heart and that you care for what I care for. I can therefore trust you with revelation, power, and intimacy."

Jesus grants revelation to His friends, sharing with them His intimate secrets and plans. He loves both sinners and sons, but He reveals the Father's heart and His most cherished purposes to those He trusts. The sloppy grace message so many promulgate today lacks the power to affect this character change. Real grace is the gift of power that asks something of us and calls us higher. Sloppy grace can bring only disappointment in the end. Hungry souls know there's more.

THE TRUTH ABOUT GRACE

All my life I've studied the people God regarded as friends and wondered why and how they had such a depth of intimacy with Him. These people received revelations of God's nature and purposes that changed the course of the world. What was it that made them trustworthy in the eyes of God when others were denied such a place? At the risk of creating offense, let me destroy some old misunderstandings about grace, the nature of God, and the Bible.

Many of us have been taught that the Old Testament is about law and the New Testament is about grace. We were told that the two are somehow set in opposition, or in contrast, to each other. This is grievous error. The same unchanging God inspired both Testaments. From the very beginning God revealed Himself as a God of grace. He was the same in the Book of Acts on Pentecost as He was in the Book of Genesis at the moment He commanded, "Let there be light" (Gen. 1:3). As the extension of His nature, His Word remains as consistent and unchanging as His person.

For this reason the apostle Paul strongly affirmed that from the beginning salvation came on the basis of faith and never stemmed from performance or obedience to the Law:

> What then shall we say that Abraham, our forefather according to the flesh, has found? For if Abraham was justified by works, he has something to boast about, but not before God. For

what does the Scripture say? "Abraham believed
God, and it was credited to him as righteousness."

—ROMANS 4:1–3

Abraham attained salvation by his faith, as a gift of
God's grace. You might ask, "What role then did the
cross play, since Jesus had not yet died?"

The answer comes in Hebrews 11: "Now faith is the
assurance of things hoped for, the conviction of things
not seen. For by it the men of old gained approval"
(vv. 1–2). The writer of Hebrews then included a long list
of those who exercised faith in God by their deeds and
concluded, "All these died in faith, without receiving
the promises, but having seen them and having welcomed them from a distance, and having confessed that
they were strangers and exiles on the earth" (v. 13). And
again, "And all these, having gained approval through
their faith, did not receive what was promised, because
God had provided something better for us, so that apart
from us they would not be made perfect" (vv. 39–40).

Simply stated, the author taught that the cross of Jesus
Christ stands for all time for all who have believed in
faith. He is saying that those who lived before the revelation of Jesus attained salvation because they hoped in
the promise of God, even though they couldn't yet see it
or know whom it would be. Because the content of the
promise was the revelation of Jesus, His sacrifice for sin
on the cross, and His resurrection, their faith and hope
saved them because it was Jesus they hoped in without
knowing it was Him. The cross of Jesus Christ stands
as the centerpiece of history, reaching both backward

and forward in time to redeem all those who trust in the promise.

Jesus never set aside or invalidated the Old Testament in any way. He didn't need to. Rather, He fulfilled its promise. Never did He say that the Old Testament was no longer valid. In fact, He commanded us not to nullify any part of it and declared that any who did would be called least in the kingdom of heaven. "Whoever then annuls one of the least of these commandments, and teaches others to do the same, shall be called least in the kingdom of heaven; but whoever keeps and teaches them, he shall be called great in the kingdom of heaven" (Matt. 5:19).

Jesus objected to all the layers, the rules, and the rules about rules that the Pharisees added to the Law, thinking that in doing so they were protecting it. He grieved that they had missed the heart of God's commandments, which were given to ensure love and well-being. He opposed the Pharisees' misapplication of Scripture, their misunderstanding and misrepresentation of the Father's heart, and the volumes of laws and regulations they added to it.

But He did not oppose the Law itself. He hated it that obedience to their concept of the Law had become a means of establishing righteousness by human effort and of earning salvation by it. It offended Him that this had been allowed to obscure the love that His Father had written into every line of it. Behind every commandment stood a principle of love that was meant for the peace and well-being of the people. The Pharisees had missed the Father's heart.

All of this explains why the apostle John wrote, "For

the Law was given through Moses; grace and truth were *realized* through Jesus Christ" (John 1:17, emphasis added). He did not say that grace and truth were not in the Law, nor did He say that grace and truth were *established* through Jesus, as if grace and truth were some new thing. He said grace and truth were *realized* in Jesus. The word for "realized" in the original Greek carries the sense of "having come into a new state of being," not that it didn't previously exist.

GRACE IS ETERNAL

In 2 Timothy 1:9–10 Paul wrote that God "has saved us and called us with a holy calling, not according to our works, but according to His own purpose and grace which was granted us in Christ Jesus *from all eternity,* but *now has been revealed* by the appearing of our Savior Christ Jesus, who abolished death and brought life and immortality to light through the gospel" (emphasis added). Grace and truth have been God's way from all eternity, from the beginning of time, from Old Testament to New Testament, because God never changes. The new covenant of grace in the blood of Jesus did not set aside or negate the Old Testament. That's a misunderstanding of what the New Testament means when it says we are not under law but under grace.

By embodying the heart of His loving Father God, Jesus destroyed wrong understandings of God's law and God's Word and made the truth and the heart of it manifest. He revealed the true meaning of what we call the Old Testament in His life and in His sacrifice.

Salvation was always by grace, and God's heart was always love. The men and women of faith, therefore, who lived before Jesus, and thus before the finished work of the cross, hoped in the promise, not knowing that the promise was Jesus. Doing so made them friends of God. They were saved because it was Jesus they hoped in, even though they didn't yet know that it would be Jesus who embodied the promise. The effect of the cross transcends time and stands for all who have faith in Him.

We must hold two truths simultaneously. First, we become His friends if we do what He commands us. This speaks to the issue of friendship and intimacy, not legalism or salvation. Many who relate to the Lord as slaves are genuinely saved, but He has called us to pass from being slaves who don't know what the Master is doing into life as sons and daughters who know and receive His love.

Even more, however, He invites us to rise higher. He bids us to become His friends who enjoy His intimate counsel and to whom He grants revelation to understand His purposes in all His words and acts.

The second truth is that all of this comes by grace, undeserved. We cannot perform perfectly. Our obedience will always be flawed, but that is why He sacrificed Himself for us.

Why does Scripture deem King David a man after God's own heart—another way of saying he was God's friend—while painting his predecessor, King Saul, as a failure? Why did God bless David to father a dynasty that resulted in the birth of Jesus centuries later, while Saul suffered disqualification? David died in bed, full of honor; Saul committed suicide after defeat in battle.

Why? David wins the contest for committing the most heinous sins, so how could he be called the man after God's own heart while Saul was not?

First, God has always been about grace. Second, it's all about the condition of the heart. We know that God looks on the heart, but what does He look for? (See 1 Samuel 16:7.) What makes a friend a friend? Isn't a friend someone you can trust? Wouldn't that be why Jesus said, "You are My friends if you do what I command you" (John 15:14)? So what about the times when I *fail* to do what He commands? What happens when I stumble in some way?

The answer lies in Psalm 51:17. "The sacrifices of God are a broken spirit; a broken and a contrite heart, O God, You will not despise." You need to be contrite only when you've failed. *Broken* means that you're more concerned and grieved for the damage you did to others than for what your error cost you personally. God trusts the broken heart. Repentance heals the wound inflicted by betrayal and restores trust, while grace paves the way.

WHAT WAS SAUL'S MISTAKE?

Here's the story. Saul failed on two counts. In 1 Samuel 13 he faced an overwhelming force of Philistines. Greatly outnumbered and growing ever more nervous, Saul received a command through Samuel to wait seven days for him to return and offer up sacrifice before battle. As seven days came and went and Samuel failed to appear, Saul's army began to scatter. Saul then defied the command to wait and offered up the sacrifice presumptuously, when he had no priestly authority to do so:

But Samuel said, "What have you done?" And Saul said, "Because I saw that the people were scattering from me, and that you did not come within the appointed days, and that the Philistines were assembling at Michmash, therefore I said, 'Now the Philistines will come down against me at Gilgal, and I have not asked the favor of the LORD.' So I forced myself and offered the burnt offering." Samuel said to Saul, "You have acted foolishly; you have not kept the commandment of the LORD your God, which He commanded you, for now the LORD would have established your kingdom over Israel forever. But now your kingdom shall not endure. The LORD has sought out for Himself a man after His own heart, and the LORD has appointed him as ruler over His people, because you have not kept what the LORD commanded you."

—1 SAMUEL 13:11–14

Confronted with his sin, Saul could offer only excuses and justifications. In 1 Samuel 15 Saul led Israel to war against the Amalekites. The command God gave in verse 3 was, "Strike Amalek and utterly destroy all that he has, and do not spare him; but put to death both man and woman, child and infant, ox and sheep, camel and donkey." Verse 9, however, records the compromise: "But Saul and the people spared Agag and the best of the sheep, the oxen, the fatlings, the lambs, and all that was good, and were not willing to destroy them utterly; but everything despised and worthless, that they utterly destroyed."

As before, when Samuel confronted him with his disobedience, Saul could offer only excuses and justifications:

> Then Saul said to Samuel, "I did obey the voice of the LORD, and went on the mission on which the LORD sent me, and have brought back Agag the king of Amalek, and have utterly destroyed the Amalekites. But the people took some of the spoil, sheep and oxen, the choicest of the things devoted to destruction, to sacrifice to the LORD your God at Gilgal."
>
> —1 SAMUEL 15:20–21

Hardly a contrite and broken heart! No wonder God had told Samuel in verse 11, "I regret that I have made Saul king, for he has turned back from following Me and has not carried out My commands." Although God loved him, Saul showed himself not to be a friend who could be trusted. His unbroken heart and lack of concern for the wounded heart of God cost him his destiny.

True friendship rests on trust. That's the issue in Jesus's statement, "You are My friends if you do what I command you." He was saying, "I can trust you with intimacy. I can trust you with My power. I can trust You with My counsel and with knowledge of My plans."

But it's always about grace, not performance. We fail. Does failure by itself have the power to disqualify us as friends of God? No! The broken heart and contrite spirit demonstrate a selfless concern for God's desires and how He feels, thus restoring trust and sealing the breach in the relationship. It's as simple as a genuine expression of, "I'm so sorry I hurt You." No excuses. No justifications. God honors and trusts one who can genuinely approach Him in that spirit after a failure.

In the natural, love for a son will never die no matter what he does, but the gift of trust is something reserved for a friend. I wouldn't trust my household to a slave or a hireling because that person would not know or carry my heart. With a friend, however, I will share my most intimate secrets. A friend carries the same heart and care for my house and family that I would. This is what God seeks.

A HEART AFTER GOD

When Saul failed, therefore, God sent Samuel to anoint David as king. David had God's heart. Embedded in the Psalms we find his love songs to God. They reveal David as a worshipper long before he became king. He sought intimacy with God, and he found it.

As king, David shared God's love for the nation. For David, life was all about God and His passion for the people of Israel. Therefore the Lord prospered him and ultimately blessed him to unite the tribes and build a great kingdom. David, however, failed miserably in a manner much worse than Saul:

> Now when evening came David arose from his bed and walked around on the roof of the king's house, and from the roof he saw a woman bathing; and the woman was very beautiful in appearance.
> —2 SAMUEL 11:2

At the end of the day in the ancient Middle East, people retreated to the flat rooftops to cool off. Bathsheba knew this. She knew, as well, that David's roof rose higher than hers and he could look down and see clearly whatever was happening. It would seem that, knowing David would be there at the end of the day, she decided to bathe herself on her roof in full view of his wandering eyes. It's like the shower scene in a bad movie in which everyone is intended to see that magnificent naked body "accidentally." It could be fairly assumed, therefore, that Bathsheba tempted David deliberately, and he chose not to look away. Was it just that once, or did he know that she would be there at a certain time every evening?

If you knew a beautiful woman would be walking naked past her open window at a certain time every night, how many of you men would say to your wife, "Honey, I'm going to walk the dog; I'll be back in thirty minutes," and you'd fool yourself into believing that you really were just walking the dog? I believe that was, in effect, why David was on the roof gazing down at Bathsheba bathing herself. He knew she'd be there because everyone went to the rooftops at the end of the day. Tempted by her beauty and knowing that she was another man's wife, he sent for her anyway.

When their illicit tryst resulted in a pregnancy, David covered his tracks. He manipulated the battle in which Uriah, Bathsheba's husband, was engaged by ordering him exposed to the worst of the fighting, hoping he would be killed. The result was as planned, and Uriah died. When the prophet Nathan confronted David with his adultery and murder, his response said it all, where his heart was concerned. "Then David said to Nathan, 'I have sinned against the LORD.' And Nathan said to

David, 'The LORD also has taken away your sin; you shall not die'" (2 Sam. 12:13).

Realization of the depth of his crime ignited David's concern for the heart of God and the wounding his sin inflicted. In contrast with Saul's response—without selfish concern for the price he would personally pay for the transgression and offering no excuses or justifications—David owned his guilt and the damage he had done. That's the heart of a friend.

First, therefore, it's always been about grace. Second, a friend has a broken and contrite heart toward the friend he has wounded. David could have protested: "But she was there tempting me. I couldn't help myself! And my other wives weren't giving me what I needed!"

Although David's offense was much worse than Saul's, the way he dealt with it was profoundly different. Saul's life ended in suicide, and his dynasty died with him. David remained king and fathered a dynasty that resulted in the birth of Jesus. At the end of his life he remained the man after God's own heart: a friend.

Two components made that a reality: (1) in failure he carried a broken and contrite spirit, and (2) he never lost his heart to obey God. Because of that heart God trusted David, and it was always about grace.

MOVING PAST FAILURE

I wish I'd personally known the apostle Peter because he comforts me. Reading of his life, I sometimes just want to say, "What a doofus!" I like him because in a number of ways I'm at least as challenged as he was.

In John 21 Jesus has been crucified and resurrected.

He has appeared physically to the disciples. Apparently stressed out from the events of recent days and still smarting from his failure in denying the Lord, Peter has illegally abandoned his calling and gone back to his old profession of fishing. To make matters worse, he has taken others with him, when he was supposed to be the leader. In Bible culture, when called to follow a prophet, the disciple left everything and understood that he could never go back. We see this in Elisha, who killed his oxen and burned the yokes (1 Kings 19:20–21). Bridges to the past life had to be burned.

After they had fished all night and caught nothing, Jesus showed up on the shore. He was like my wife, who caught our oldest daughter at the theater after she had been grounded to her room. Peter got so excited, or fearfully convicted, that he put his clothes *on* to jump in the lake and swim to shore. Brain not functioning! When they all had come to shore, Jesus ate a meal with them, prepared on the fire He had already built.

After breakfast the confrontation began, and it wasn't pretty. "So when they had finished breakfast, Jesus said to Simon Peter, 'Simon, son of John, do you love Me more than these?' He said to Him, 'Yes, Lord; You know that I love You.' He said to him, 'Tend My lambs'" (John 21:15). Jesus asked if Peter loved Him with *agape*, or "covenant" love. Peter answered that he loved Jesus with *philos*, or "friendship" love. Jesus wanted to know if Peter cared for what belonged to Him as if it were his own, as would a true friend.

Twice Jesus asked the same question. Twice Peter gave the same answer. "Yes, Lord, I'm Your friend." Twice

Jesus exhorted him to tend His lambs. Apparently Peter failed to understand the meaning of *friend*.

On the third try Jesus used Peter's own word *phileo* (the verbal form), as if to say, "OK, well then, are you really My friend?" It was the ultimate insult. In the culture of Bible times to ask a question once was acceptable. To ask the same question a second time constituted an insult, but to ask a third time was the equivalent of a backhanded slap in the face. Desperate for the restoration of His friend, Jesus sought to wake Peter up to his calling in the most forceful way He knew.

The content of it had to sound something like this: "If you feel that way about Me, if you really are My friend, then obey My command and feed My sheep. Repent of this violation, pick up your calling, and go back to work caring for the things I care for." Jesus looked for a heart that cared for what He cared for.

Doesn't this sound a lot like, "You are My friends if you do what I command you"? Throughout this difficult encounter Jesus sought to win His friend. Notice once more that grace is always available for failure when the sinner responds with a broken and contrite spirit.

Jesus confronted Peter harshly in love, and Peter's heart broke. After all, it was the second serious betrayal he had committed in a matter of just weeks. Repentance and restoration came as he resumed his calling and led the early church into Pentecost and persecution. To be amazed at the intimate revelation Jesus gave to His friend Peter, you have only to read the books of 1 Peter and 2 Peter.

GRACE IS ALWAYS AVAILABLE

Obedience has always been a crucial element of friendship with God, but He has always given grace for failure. This is how it is with God's friends whose hearts He trusts to be broken for His sake when failure inevitably comes. I don't want to merely be *loved* by God. I want to be *trusted* by God as His friend, and I know that God wants to trust me. He therefore adjusts me sometimes, just as He did Peter, changing me without condemning me or throwing me away. He needs only my broken and contrite heart.

Grace never means that it's all OK, that He leaves me as I am because the cross is a finished work, and He did it all. The cross ensures my salvation, but it doesn't change my character unless I cooperate with and embrace it. God's friends embrace change. "If I'm His friend, then I have His heart; and if I have His heart, then I know what He knows and love what He loves."

Let's no longer misrepresent the Old Testament as law and the New Testament as grace. It was always grace. God kept trusting David in his failure, requiring only his brokenness in the face of sin. Peter remained Jesus's friend, trusted with the leadership of the early church, even when he had fallen down. He had only to repent and share Jesus's heart for people.

The Book of James has never been popular with grace teachers, but only because they miss the point in this foundational passage:

> Was not Abraham our father justified by works
> when he offered up Isaac his son on the altar? You

see that faith was working with his works, and as a result of the works, faith was perfected; and the Scripture was fulfilled which says, "And Abraham believed God, and it was reckoned to him as righteousness," and he was called the friend of God. You see that a man is justified by works and not by faith alone.

—JAMES 2:21–24

Friendship cannot happen in a vacuum. The deepest love and intimacy are built when two parties sacrifice together, paying a price together for a great purpose beyond themselves. A friend feels in himself the heart of his friend.

Abraham's willingness to sacrifice Isaac was a kind of foreshadowing, as well as a type, of Father God's sacrifice of His only Son, Jesus, to die for us. On the verge of plunging the knife into Isaac's heart, Abraham felt what God feels. He understood God's anguish in sacrificing Jesus millennia later, and in that shared experience he became God's friend.

My own son, who serves as my co-pastor, becomes more than my son—he becomes my friend—when I can trust him with the flock I serve and love. I know that he focuses his heart beyond himself and his personal need, that he gives his care and his love to the things that matter to me. When he fails, I know his heart breaks and that he does what must be done to heal the wound and restore trust. Because this is the heart of what our Father in heaven asks of us, I ask nothing less of those I call my friends on earth.

Grace lies in the fact that my friendship with God isn't based on the perfection of my performance but on the brokenness of my heart toward Him. Abraham failed. To save his own skin, he gave his wife into the harem of a foreign king. Despairing of the promise of a son through Sarah, he took Sarah's maid and fathered an illegitimate child. David failed when he couldn't keep his pants zipped and then committed adultery and murder to hide his failure. Peter abandoned his calling.

Nevertheless, each of them was a trusted friend of God. Why? The broken heart in clean and pure repentance made them trustworthy. Ultimately they cared for what God cares for and at high cost to themselves. How deeply do you and I care for what God feels? When a friend hurts, I hurt. I feel it inside of me, as my own hurt. Am I that way with God?

Can we move beyond use and abuse of our Lord, taking salvation for granted, and learn to feel what He feels? When He hurts, do we hurt? Does what blesses Him bless us? When we see a messed-up, broken, and lost individual, do we see what Jesus sees? Would we have seen the disciple inside the tax-collecting Roman collaborator? Would we have seen what Jesus loved in the unclean and immoral woman who came into the Pharisee's home to wash His feet? Would we have seen the potential evangelist in the immoral Samaritan woman at the well who had been married five times and was living with someone she was not married to? Every man in town knew her. No respectable woman would befriend her.

I often pray: "Lord! Would You trust us with another pulse of Your revival Spirit and power even though we blew it in the past? We didn't really understand, but You've labored long over us and we've said, 'Yes, Lord, change us.' Would You trust us once more to be stewards of a great outpouring?" Can we be His friends? I have learned to be a son of God. I am becoming His friend. When that happens, something changes so deep inside as to leave no room for disappointment. My heart is full!

Chapter 7

SHIFTING TO A KINGDOM MENTALITY

———— ✦ ————

The fact that the coming of the kingdom of God to Earth was the central proclamation of Jesus's ministry is no great theological secret. Have we, however, really understood and properly applied all that He meant? If we have, then why is there this growing sense of dissatisfaction and disappointment among so many believers who love Jesus and the ministry of His Spirit? Why do we not see more fruit of the kingdom? Perhaps the answer lies in a deficient understanding of what the kingdom of God really means.

As the first prophet to arise after four hundred years of prophetic silence, John the Baptist proclaimed the coming of the kingdom of God in preparation for Jesus's ministry. His message? "Repent, for the kingdom of heaven is at hand" (Matt. 3:2). Mark quoted him a little differently: "The time is fulfilled, and the kingdom of God is at hand; repent and believe in the gospel" (Mark 1:15). John announced the coming kingdom of God, called people to prepare for it, and then recognized it in Jesus when he saw Him coming for baptism.

Following Jesus's baptism at John's hand, the Holy Spirit drove Him into the wilderness to be tempted by the devil forty days and forty nights. When He returned and began His earthly ministry, He picked up where John left off: "From that time Jesus began to preach and say, 'Repent, for the kingdom of heaven is at hand'" (Matt. 4:17). Later, according to Mark, Jesus issued a promise: "Truly I say to you, there are some of those who are standing here who will not taste death until they see the kingdom of God after it has come with power" (Mark 9:1).

Matthew summarized the progress of Jesus's ministry in a single sentence: "Jesus was going throughout all Galilee, teaching in their synagogues and proclaiming the gospel of the kingdom, and healing every kind of disease and every kind of sickness among the people" (Matt. 4:23). Proclamation with demonstration has always been the biblical pattern.

Jesus, expressing the heart of the Lord's Prayer in Matthew 6:9–10, said in the first two sentences, "Pray, then, in this way: 'Our Father who is in heaven, hallowed be Your name. Your kingdom come. Your will be done, on earth as it is in heaven.'"

These represent just a few, a very few, of the New Testament references to the kingdom of God. After a while you might begin to think, "Doesn't Jesus have any other message?" The answer would be no, that not a single word He spoke lacked a connection to the message of the kingdom. He told parables to illustrate how it works. He spoke of it in terms of who would be allowed to enter. He talked about how it's received. He articulated its character and nature in the Sermon on the Mount (Matt. 5–7), with all of its rich teaching on humility, gentleness, hunger for righteousness, promises to those who are persecuted, and reward for those who grieve over the lost condition of the world and the suffering around them. He demonstrated its reality with signs and wonders of God's mercy.

The message never varied. The kingdom of God is here. The kingdom of God has come. In everything He said and did, Jesus maintained that single drumbeat. In Him the kingdom of God came among us, and in the gift of the Holy Spirit on the Day of Pentecost, the power of it manifested in and through the early church and remains available to all of us today.

All of this means that God calls us to develop a culture of the kingdom that flows from a deep and intimate relationship with the Father through Jesus. Not even the writers of Scripture could find adequate words to describe what must be realized inside of each of us for such a culture to take root and thrive. Language serves to point us toward the kingdom of God but cannot fully express it. In a sense we must be born again—and again, and again, and again. The evidence of such a rebirth can be observed, but its substance will ever remain a mystery, as Jesus said: "The wind blows where it wishes and you hear the sound of it, but do not know where it comes from and where it is going; so is everyone who is born of the Spirit" (John 3:8).

Unable to find language adequate to express the full heart of the kingdom of God, Jesus therefore embodied the kingdom of God in Himself and prayed that the disciples would catch it through relationship with Him: "He who has seen Me has seen the Father" (John 14:9). We catch it in just the same way.

Greater Works

"Truly, truly, I say to you, he who believes in Me, the works that I do, he will do also; and greater works than these he will do; because I go to the Father" (John 14:12). Too often you and I go to conferences to try to learn how to be supernatural. We study methods for moving God's hand to heal people. We try to figure out how to hear His voice. We sometimes think we can obtain all of that for ourselves through some gifted human being who lays hands on us and imparts it to us. Unfortunately, in all that effort, we miss the depth of the reality of the kingdom. Disappointment results.

The force of Jesus's words in John 14:9 might go something like this: "I'm not giving you a method. I'm giving you a relationship. I go to the Father, and because I go to the Father, you'll do greater things than I did." Jesus takes us with Him into a relationship of oneness with the Father that mirrors His own, praying for us: "That they may all be one; even as You, Father, are in Me and I in You, that they also may be in Us" (John 17:21), and, "I in them and You in Me" (v. 23).

We long for the promised greater works and puzzle over why we don't see them. Certainly we do see miracles, but "greater works" are seldom, if ever, witnessed. So-called faith teachers tell us that the causal factor for the greater works is some mysterious quantity of faith that most of us never achieve (and then carry guilt for our lack). We miss what Jesus actually said and then come away empty, having fished in the wrong pond. In the name of faith we turn from salvation by faith alone and make faith itself into a work until the effort results in spiritual fatigue and erosion of hope. Many just give up and settle for something less than the promise.

Faith connects us with Jesus in relationship, but the causal element of "greater works" lies not in our ability to generate a state of emotional certainty or trust but in a healthy relationship with the Father through Jesus. Jesus clearly promised greater works because, He said, "I go to the Father," not because we believe. This relieves us of the burden of human effort to generate enough faith to make something happen, and it roots us where we belong in the intimacy and freedom of a relationship with the Father who loves us. Stop seeking the supernatural and focus on intimacy with Father God. The result will be much more satisfying.

In a relationship of intimacy with Jesus and the Father, when the Holy Spirit moves, we move with Him. "Whatever you ask in My name, that will I do, so that the Father may be glorified in the Son" (John 14:13). In other words, in the truest sense of acting in Jesus's name, when you accurately represent Him before the Father and when your heart is one with His, He responds. Far from giving us a method, He gives us a living relationship of intimacy.

This relationship with the Father through Jesus lies at the heart of the kingdom of God. In seeking the kingdom, you may be looking for something you can understand with your mind and control in your life, but

Jesus offers a relationship, the nature of which remains a mystery you can neither understand nor control.

Satisfaction for the hunger we feel cannot be found in methods, confessions, ritual prayers, impartations, or any other form of purely human effort. We must seek the depth and innocent simplicity of the relationship we've been offered. Do this, and disappointment will become a thing of the past. It's the end of striving. In relationship we rest.

A MENTAL SHIFT

To establish a culture of the kingdom of God, a significant mentality shift must take deep root among as many of us as will receive it. "Do not worry then, saying, 'What will we eat?' or 'What will we drink?' or 'What will we wear for clothing?' For the Gentiles eagerly seek all these things; for your heavenly Father knows that you need all these things" (Matt. 6:31–32). These verses describe aspects of the self-obsessed culture in which we live and in which the kingdom of God cannot thrive.

When God's people allow themselves to become absorbed with concern for those things to the point that they are a focus, it becomes proportionately more difficult to experience, understand, or move in the power of the kingdom of God. At some level too many of us ask, "How can I get what I want or need on this earth?"—and a plethora of teachers are lined up to tell us how to accomplish that: "With health, wealth, and happiness!" Wrong focus! We can never get there by starting with that.

Better to ask myself, "*Why* do I want to prosper

financially?" Is it so that I won't have to worry? Is it so I can get that house I've always wanted? Maybe I want to take the pressure off myself and pay down my debt. Or, better, do I wish to prosper so that in some way I can shine for the kingdom of God beyond myself to manifest the will of God for others to see? Is it so I can contribute more to what God wants to do?

Why do I want to be healed of that physical problem? Is it so I won't hurt anymore? Or is it so the truth of who God is can be manifested in me so that the kingdom of God will be realized in a way that all can see? Is it the goal of my life that there must be nothing in me to hinder the flow of the kingdom of God through me? Is it about me or about the kingdom?

Why do I seek counseling? Is it so I can be selfishly relieved of my hurt? Or is it so my character can be cleansed and changed in order that nothing in or through me fails to reflect the nature of Jesus? Is it so nothing unclean comes out of me so that I can minister more effectively beyond myself for the sake of others?

Do I desire the power and the gift of healing so that I can see something supernatural and be amazed by it? Is it so that I personally can be seen as gifted and important? Or is it really to advance God's will being done on this earth in mercy to others?

I'm convinced that this shift of mentality goes deeper than most of us realize. The culture of the world has captivated our lives in ways and at depths to which most of us are functionally blind. The character of the kingdom manifests in the cross and resurrection of Jesus, drawing us beyond ourselves in every aspect of life.

SEEK THE KINGDOM

Most of us learned this verse in Sunday school or at least heard it somewhere: "Seek first His kingdom and His righteousness, and all these things will be added to you" (Matt. 6:33). A full, true understanding of Jesus's words in this verse comes from looking at its two parts.

Seek first His kingdom. This points us toward His will and the manifestation of His love and character on the earth. Whatever I'm doing, I must be doing it to see the kingdom of God manifest in and through me. I must live focused on seeing His will and His mercy flowing through me and through those with whom I walk. I want to see the nature of my Lord made visible in power and purity on the earth.

All these things will be added to you. This does not mean you should seek the kingdom first *so that* all these things will be added to you, and that if you don't, then all these things will *not* be added to you. Jesus never engaged in religious manipulation, nor did He give us a magic button to push. He gave us a relationship. He was saying that we are free to seek the kingdom as a first priority *because* all these things are *already* added to us. Our loving heavenly Father provides for His children in a way that frees them to live a different way: selflessly for a golden and eternal purpose beyond themselves.

Context determines meaning. The previous verses undergird what I'm saying. Here is the context:

> And why are you worried about clothing? Observe how the lilies of the field grow; they do not toil nor do they spin, yet I say to you that not even

Solomon in all his glory clothed himself like one of these. But if God so clothes the grass of the field, which is alive today and tomorrow is thrown into the furnace, will He not much more clothe you? You of little faith! Do not worry then, saying, "What will we eat?" or "What will we drink?" or "What will we wear for clothing?" For the Gentiles eagerly seek all these things; for your heavenly Father knows that you need all these things.
—MATTHEW 6:28–32

Because God has already provided for your material needs, you have been freed to seek the kingdom first and fulfill your destiny in the service of God and others. "Life is a drag, then you die" is the world's lie. Your worldly job is not your destiny. It's merely the funding source for your ministry, God's provision for living and giving. Your destiny lies in the manner in which you carry yourself in the character of the Father as you manifest the kingdom of God in the place where you work. Your truest calling lies in affecting other people with a revelation of the goodness of God.

The second key component of Matthew 6:33 is the command to seek "His righteousness," the character change that transforms my nature to conform to His. I long for intimacy with God, to have His heart in me so that through me the kingdom of God can be seen and understood. I long for my Father and my Savior to be accurately represented in all that they are through me and through those who walk with me.

That requires a mentality shift, a dramatic and sweeping change of focus. I don't want to be absorbed in trying to make healing happen. I want to be focused on intimacy with the One who heals. I don't want to be consumed with trying to make people feel good. Let the motivational speakers who pretend to preach the gospel do that. I want to be focused on Jesus Christ and Him crucified (1 Cor. 2:2) because I want the level of selflessness and love I see on that cross to become the hallmark of my life. In that lies the heart of the kingdom of God.

If this is the focus that becomes real inside us, then the goodness of it will unfold in all our relationships. Families will be restored. Children will be reconciled with parents, and tangible manifestations of God's power will become the order of the day. People who never knew the Lord will commit their lives to Him because they experience the kingdom in and through us.

In the kingdom of God we're pursuing a relationship with God that changes our nature. Miracles will follow, but they'll be the result, not the focus. The focus will rest on the presence of God and who He is in us until we all truly know that the Lord is God.

ROOTED IN COVENANT

God's righteousness, His character, and His perfection have always been covenant-based. His covenant of commitment to us cannot be broken. As I seek to reflect that element of His kingdom and character in my own life, I must ask whether my relationships are in good shape. Why am I in them? Is it for me? Or is it for the kingdom of God? Am I in relationship with people for my personal benefit, for how they make me feel, or for what they can do for me? Or is it so that the kingdom of

God can be revealed on Earth regardless of the prospect of any benefit to me?

I have relationships that are easy, and I have some that are difficult. All of my "easy" relationships are covenant relationships, but not all of my covenant relationships are easy. How then must my heart be changed? There are people to whom I give my life because it's not difficult to do. They make it easy. Others are not so easy. I, therefore, bind myself in covenant to the difficult ones because it's the kingdom thing to do in spite of the fact that they give me a royal pain in the backside: "For the love of Christ controls us" (2 Cor. 5:14). I am compelled to do this because it's the heart of my God who loves each of us with a depth of grace not conditioned on the performance of the ones He loves.

This calls for a deep shift of emphasis. As we discussed in the last chapter, three times Jesus commanded Peter in John 21, "Feed My sheep!" (vv. 15–17). He meant: "Get out of yourself, Peter. Put the kingdom first, loving others first, ministering the love of the Father first, and go take care of My people. Be poured out for them!"

We must cultivate a culture of the kingdom reflecting the heart and character of God; a collective mind shift, a fresh mentality, a different way of thinking and living. What's our focus? Do you understand what you're really asking when you pray, "Your kingdom come, Your will be done"?

WORKING AS A TEAM

If you've ever been part of an athletic team, you know that team mentality is everything and can mean the difference between winning and losing. This mentality has a lot to do with attitude about the game and with what the players believe about themselves, one another, and their coach. Every team has its own culture that determines whether or not it becomes a winning team.

Do you remember the 2004 Olympics in Athens, Greece, when the United States continued its tradition started in the 1992 Olympics of fielding a dream team made up of our best basketball professionals? They came into Athens with an arrogant attitude and played like a gang of individual superstars who were in it for themselves, instead of developing a team culture and cohesion. As a result, it didn't matter how gifted any of them were individually. As a team they got creamed by lesser-talent teams and earned the nickname "the Nightmare Team."

It's the same with the body of Christ and the coming of the kingdom of God. The culture of the kingdom begins with an attitude in which we approach life and one another. It defines how we relate to the coach, who just happens to be God, and it determines our focus as we move toward the goal. Am I really playing to maximize my brothers and sisters so that we all reach the goal together, or is it ultimately all about me?

A culture is a group of people who belong to one another, who identify with one another; and it takes more than you alone for the fruit of that kind of mindset to manifest itself, even in your personal life. It requires all of us being in it together, encouraging one another, reinforcing one another, and seeking the Lord together. If the team loses, you lose personally. If the team wins, you win individually: "And if one member suffers, all the members suffer with it; if one member is honored, all the members rejoice with it. Now you are Christ's body, and individually members of it" (1 Cor. 12:26–27).

Jesus performed miracles because of oneness with His Father. In relationship and intimacy with His Father, He knew when He was moving and moved with Him because He knew it wasn't about Him. It was about revealing the Father. The kingdom of God, therefore, calls us to demonstrate the true nature of the Father on the earth and to walk in it. Jesus told the disciples, "He who has seen Me has seen the Father" (John 14:9).

As a people together, therefore, we seek to develop a kingdom way of thinking and living until the air around us is as alive with the presence of God, as the air around Jesus was almost two thousand years ago.

GETTING THE RIGHT FOCUS

Jesus did not mean that His command to seek the kingdom of God would set us upon a quest to see miracles. Especially in renewal circles, it seems we've too often equated it with that. The miracles of the kingdom begin, not with a desire for miracles, but with the Father's compassion for people flowing through us:

> Seeing the people, He felt compassion for them, because they were distressed and dispirited like sheep without a shepherd... Jesus summoned His twelve disciples and gave them authority over unclean spirits, to cast them out, and to heal every kind of disease and every kind of sickness.
> —MATTHEW 9:36; 10:1

Here we see the Father's heart of mercy and love revealed on Earth through His disciples. Miracles were the by-product.

A kingdom mentality focuses not on self and personal need for fulfillment. The heart of the kingdom of heaven is compassion, the Father's love, and concern for those we touch. It's the reach beyond ourselves. It requires that we seek intimacy with the Father and become in our character what He is in His love. Miracles and experiences of the supernatural will be the result, not the goal, but in a true kingdom mentality we understand that we can only go there together.

The very existence of the disappointment and frustration so many of us feel tells me a hunger is growing that positions us on the verge of entering a reality of the kingdom of God that most of us have never seen or known. When this happens, we'll be amazed at both the supernatural intervention of God we'll see in every aspect of our lives and our impact on the world around us.

We must come into this together because it won't work for us one at a time. It's a culture that nurtures the individual, but it's not a private, individual thing. This is why we're alive. This is what we were born for. God has ordained a destiny for us in the kingdom of God. He will manifest the truth of who He is as destiny flows from the intimacy with Him that all of us who hunger for Him will come to know.

Chapter 8

THE FRUIT OF THE
BARREN WOMB

———•———

A s a pastor, I listen to the hearts of the saints. I
hear their hurts, aches, pains, disappointments,
and fears—and I feel them as my own. These days, from
too many people, I hear and feel erosion of hope, much
of which comes as a result of delayed promises. God
hears and feels this as well, but His good purposes lie
behind every delay of promise. This chapter speaks to a
revival of hope.

Four women grace the pages of Scripture whose
wombs God closed but whose stories come to us laden
with lessons about the heart of God and the ways in
which He chooses to work. Sarah (Abraham's wife) lived
as a barren woman into her old age. Rachel (Jacob's wife)
suffered as her less attractive sister bore children while
she could not. Hannah (mother of the prophet Samuel)
suffered the taunts of her husband's other wife as she
lived year to year without a child. Elizabeth (mother of
John the Baptist in the New Testament) suffered, as did

her ancestral mother Sarah. Each of these women lived under a cloud of deep despair and anguish of soul.

In Bible times a woman who could not bear a child was thought to be cursed. Her whole purpose and value as a person in that culture revolved around her ability to reproduce. If she couldn't conceive and bear a child— especially a son—she would be looked down upon and despised by her community. Even friends and family would believe that something was wrong with her, that there must have been hidden sin somewhere in her life. She would suffer utter devastation of heart and spirit.

Barrenness, the unfruitful womb, makes a fitting metaphor for what a lot of us feel today. It's the sense that you can't seem to reproduce, to bear the fruit that you know God has promised. It seems like you're stuck, blocked somehow, and no matter what you do, you can't seem to move into the fullness of the Lord that you know is reserved for you.

You began with dreams and hopes for your life and ministry, but somewhere down the road they started to wane. It's been too long, you've worked so hard, and it's begun to seem as if those things you interpreted as promises will never come to pass. At some level you're tired and disappointed and want to give up. Age doesn't shield you from this—you can suffer from it when you're young, and you can suffer from it when you're old.

Maybe it was the end of the marriage you thought would last, on which you pinned so many hopes and dreams. Perhaps the children for whom you had such high hopes have rejected your faith, broken the law, or suffered some other heartbreaking disaster.

When you became a believer, God filled you with

glorious visions and promises for your life and ministry. You had a sense of destiny, anticipation, and excitement, but now too much time has passed and you feel left out, sidelined, as if you've accomplished little. The promises will never come to pass, and you no longer have the strength to sustain hope. That's barrenness!

Perhaps you've been part of a church—maybe even a leader of one—and have seen God pour out His Spirit to heal people and grant visitations of His presence and power. Yet for years on end the church seems stuck and unable to grow past a certain point. Try as you might, you can't figure out why. After all the effort and energy you've expended, it just makes no sense.

In all of this your sense of hope has been broken. "Hope deferred makes the heart sick," says Proverbs 13:12, and so you begin to feel like those women I cited at the beginning of the chapter. You wonder if maybe you're cursed. Perhaps God doesn't like you. Where is He, after all?

Two words appear in Scripture to describe how those women felt: *reproach* and *disgrace*. *Reproach* means "to speak to someone in tones of disappointment or disapproval." *Disgrace* comes to someone whose moral rectitude or value as a person has come into question.

In each of those four cases of a closed womb, through the barren woman came the child of promise—and that child became the turning point for redemptive history in his day, often after an impossibly long period of waiting. Sarah finally bore Isaac, through whom came the promise to Abraham, father of nations, and the birth of the entire nation of Israel. Rachel gave birth to Joseph, who rose to become second only to

Pharaoh over all Egypt, just in time to save his family from famine. Hannah brought the prophet Samuel into the world. Samuel carried enormous authority in Israel and anointed Israel's first two kings. Finally, the fruit of Elizabeth's womb was John the Baptist, the first prophetic voice in four hundred years and the forerunner of Jesus Himself.

Repeatedly God brings key redemption and turning points in the history of salvation through what has appeared to be the barren life. Something about the suffering that results from extended barrenness brings about the kind of character changes that prepare the way for the birth of blessing and destiny.

Pressure Exposes Our Flaws

Pressures of delayed promise have the power to expose all sorts of flaws and cracks in personalities and even families. Here are several.

Family conflict. Jealousy toward the one who has gets a foothold in the one who lacks. One family member can adopt a superior attitude toward the other because one appears to be blessed and the other doesn't. Blaming others for the pain can take root when hurt and a sense of failure develop in the one deprived.

Feelings of shame. People in and out of the family begin groping for the cause, trying to understand why this lack or failure exists. "There must be something wrong with me"; "If you'd just done it differently"; "If you would change somehow, then your life or your ministry would thrive. This barrenness is your fault."

Under the weight of this onslaught the barren one begins to crumble.

Hopelessness. In the face of delay it says: "I give up. It will never happen. I'm just marking time until I die. I'm not favored, and I never will be." Life loses its savor. Rather than live the adventure, the barren one just goes through the motions.

Loss of faith. It echoes: "I don't believe the promises of God anymore. It's just too painful. My promise will never come to me." Loss of faith can be very dangerous. I've seen people at this stage of extended barrenness reject the whole package and leave the faith altogether. Passion and purpose die.

Foolish decisions. In the effort to force God's hand and bring the promise into reality, you begin to try to make things happen in your own way, often seeking to alleviate the pain by some illegal means. You'll see that at work in the stories of these four women. In your own life you might foolishly decide to give up on fellowship and church. Temptation to return to an old bad habit may loom large. Sin takes on a heightened appeal, promising relief it can never deliver.

Keys to Redemptive Destiny

Both keys to seeing the promise of redemptive destiny fulfilled are inseparable and yet constitute separate expressions of *faithfulness*.

God's faithfulness. God is faithful to His promise. In every case the biblical record shows that God did what He said He would, even when the people involved had failed miserably.

Our faithfulness. Don't let go. The one thing that qualified these four barren women in the Bible was their faithfulness—they never stopped reaching out to God and worshipping Him. Because they stood in the face of opposition, they were in position to receive the blessing when at last it came. You can abandon faith and fellowship in the face of discouragement and lost hope, but one day you'll hear that God has sent a mighty visitation. Everything He said would come to pass will begin to unfold, but you won't be there to receive it. You'll be out of place because you weren't faithful.

Too many people confuse faithfulness with legalism or religion. Nothing could be further from the truth. Faithfulness expresses love. Among other things, love must be consistent in the face of all conditions. For those of us who hunger for more and have been waiting long to see it, faithfulness is what keeps us in position to receive. Only one hundred twenty faithful remained in the Upper Room, ready to receive when the Holy Spirit fell on the Day of Pentecost. Where were the thousands who had followed Jesus for the three and a half years before that day?

Desperate prayer. Extended barrenness brings humbling, breaks your heart, and makes you desperate for God. You therefore cry out passionately for God to bring the promise to pass, and in humility you put all your pain, disappointment, frustration, and anger into that prayer. God hears!

ABRAHAM AND SARAH'S ANGUISH

"Sarai was barren; she had no child" (Gen. 11:30). Remember what I said about shame and foolish decisions? Here it comes:

> Now Sarai, Abram's wife had borne him no children, and she had an Egyptian maid whose name was Hagar. So Sarai said to Abram, "Now behold, the LORD has prevented me from bearing children. Please go in to my maid; perhaps I will obtain children through her." And Abram listened to the voice of Sarai.
>
> —GENESIS 16:1–2

Here's when the blaming began, and it started with blaming God: "The LORD has prevented me" (v. 2). Delay of promise can lead to the ungodly belief that God has turned against you. This leads to foolish decisions when you attempt to alleviate the pain and fill the empty place by illegal means. Having grown tired of waiting, you try to make the plan of God happen by human effort rather than by God's promise.

When things born of human effort outside the plan of God fail to produce the blessing, family conflict is never far behind:

> After Abram had lived ten years in the land of Canaan, Abram's wife Sarai took Hagar the Egyptian, her maid, and gave her to her husband Abram as his wife. He went in to Hagar, and she conceived; and when she saw that she had conceived, her mistress was despised in her sight.
>
> —GENESIS 16:3–4

The servant looked down on her mistress. Conflict and division erupted as the fruit of disobedience. Only God's plans work. Nothing good can come from a plan of the flesh. These thousands of years later Israel continues to pay today for the birth of Ishmael, as his descendants battle for possession of the land, perpetuating the conflict begun between Sarai and Hagar.

Sarai initiated the trespass and then blamed Abram for the miserable outcome:

> And Sarai said to Abram, "May the wrong done me be upon you. I gave my maid into your arms, but when she saw that she had conceived, I was despised in her sight. May the LORD judge between you and me."
>
> —GENESIS 16:5

Family conflict resulted when the plan that wasn't the Lord's didn't turn out well. Does this sound familiar to anyone?

Sin, then, begets sin when plans God did not initiate work out poorly. "But Abram said to Sarai, 'Behold, your maid is in your power; do to her what is good in your sight.' So Sarai treated her harshly, and she fled from her presence" (Gen. 16:6). Yet the promise remains even in the face of sin because God has always been a God of grace:

> Then God said to Abraham, "As for Sarai your wife, you shall not call her name Sarai, but Sarah shall be her name. I will bless her, and indeed I will give you a son by her. Then I will bless her, and she shall be a mother of nations; kings of

peoples will come from her." Then Abraham fell
on his face and laughed, and said in his heart,
"Will a child be born to a man one hundred years
old? And will Sarah, who is ninety years old,
bear a child?"

—GENESIS 17:15–17

Old and wrinkled, Sarah was far past her child-
bearing years; her menstrual cycle had long since ceased.
Abraham could not accept what God had told him. Loss
of hope had rendered him incapable of believing the
promise, even when it came directly from the mouth of
God. He laughed at it.

THE DANGER OF UNGODLY PLANS

Some of us have lived long enough to think there's not
enough time left for the promises of God to come to pass.
If this describes you, you may be considering settling for
second best. So much time has passed that, in desperation, you may be turning to a plan that God has not
blessed. "And Abraham said to God, 'Oh that Ishmael
might live before You!'" (Gen. 17:18). As did Abraham, you
could begin formulating your own plans and pleading
with God to bless them in fulfillment of a promise God
gave, but God isn't interested in those kinds of plans—
the plans of men. They don't work. His do.

In the late 1980s the Lord had been trying to tell me
that the time had come for me to leave the church I
had planted in Post Falls, Idaho, and move to Denver.
For eleven years I had been fully invested in striving
to make prophetic promises over my life come to pass
through that church. Not wanting to hear what God

had planned, and feeling sick in my spirit as a result of promises delayed, I sought to make it all come to pass by opening a second service twenty minutes away in Spokane, Washington.

Of course it didn't work. I finally got the point after someone stole the sound system we had purchased for that endeavor. Some setbacks send prophetic messages! I was trying to substitute an Ishmael for God's Isaac when my heart had lost hope in the promise of God. Plans birthed in my own heart are almost always illegitimate. Plans birthed first in His heart and then inspired in mine are the ones He blesses—but sometimes He doesn't bless until after a very long period of waiting and preparation.

THE PROMISE RENEWED

God doesn't change His plans to please us. Ishmael could never be the child of promise. God, therefore, enforced His plan. "But God said, 'No, but Sarah your *wife* will bear you a son, and you shall call his name Isaac; and I will establish *My covenant* with him for an everlasting covenant for his descendants after him'" (Gen. 17:19, emphasis added). Only the legitimate plan, the one that passes God's moral standard, consistent with God's own covenant, will be blessed as the plan of promise:

> As for Ishmael, I have heard you; behold, I will bless him, and will make him fruitful and will multiply him exceedingly. He shall become the father of twelve princes, and I will make him a great nation. But My *covenant* I will establish with

Isaac, whom Sarah will bear to you at this season
next year.
—GENESIS 17:20–21, EMPHASIS ADDED

Finally, to this miserable failure of a couple, God
appeared in person. In chapter 18 three men came to
Abraham's tent who I believe were representative of
the triune God. Abraham invited them in and called
on Sarah to prepare a meal for them while he went to
butcher a calf for the dinner they would share. After the
meal these messengers of the Lord began to speak prophetically. As hungry as Abraham was for the Lord, his
faith remained broken by the delay, hurt, and rejection
he felt. For Sarah's part, the situation was worse:

> He said, "I will surely return to you at this time
> next year; and behold, Sarah your wife will have
> a son." And Sarah was listening at the tent door,
> which was behind him. Now Abraham and Sarah
> were old, advanced in age; Sarah was past child-
> bearing. Sarah laughed to herself, saying, "After I
> have become old, shall I have pleasure, my lord
> being old also?"
> —GENESIS 18:10–12

Suffering brought sarcasm. Paraphrased, she said,
"Both of us are old, and he can't even get an erection anymore. How could he possibly pleasure me?" Not even a
dramatic physical visitation from the Lord could pene-
trate her despair and the bitterness that arose from it.

Has delay so broken your faith that you no longer can
take full pleasure or encouragement either from a sense
of the Lord's presence or when God does a miracle

before your very eyes? Sarah camped on the negative, even in the face of a direct word from God:

> And the LORD said to Abraham, "Why did Sarah laugh, saying, 'Shall I indeed bear a child, when I am so old?' Is anything too difficult for the LORD? At the appointed time I will return to you, at this time next year, and Sarah will have a son." Sarah denied it however, saying, "I did not laugh"; for she was afraid. And He said, "No, but you did laugh."
> —GENESIS 18:13-15

Is that what some of us have fallen to as well?

It could seem from these verses that God loves to show off. That He loves to wait to bring fulfillment or rescue until situations seem impossible so that the miracles He chooses to perform appear even larger than they would have otherwise, and so that the lesson in faith can be driven home more deeply.

Times of delay bring about character changes. But that means God must reveal and expose your sin and unbelief. Sarah got caught and exposed in her mocking unbelief. She wasn't punished, just exposed. God will reveal to you how shallow your faith truly is.

Sarah did indeed bear Isaac, and through him the whole line of Israel came, which ultimately brought forth Jesus. Isaac, born of a barren womb, fulfilled his destiny to become a key figure in redemptive history.

RACHEL'S TORMENT

Jacob had two wives. His father-in-law, Laban, tricked him into marrying Leah, the less attractive sister, after making him serve seven years for the wife he thought would be Rachel—then forced him to serve seven more years for Rachel, the one he loved. We see that, once again, deferred hope and delay of promise produced family conflict. This time it grew out of jealousy because God seemed to favor one above the other:

> Now the LORD saw that Leah was unloved, and He opened her womb, but Rachel was barren... Now when Rachel saw that she bore Jacob no children, she became jealous of her sister; and she said to Jacob, "Give me children, or else I die."
>
> —GENESIS 29:31; 30:1

Again, looking for someone to blame in her pain, the wife lays it on the husband: "Give me children, or else I die." In other words, "The promise has not come to pass, and I'm unhappy because of you." Yes, it's irrational, but pain can do that. She hurt so badly that if her hope failed to come to fulfillment, she would rather die.

From the hurt and anger, bad decision-making resulted. "Then Jacob's anger burned against Rachel, and he said, 'Am I in the place of God, who has withheld from you the fruit of the womb?'" (Gen. 30:2). When the pain of unfulfilled hope grows large enough, stupid decisions follow. "She said, 'Here is my maid Bilhah, go in to her that she may bear on my knees, that through her I too may have children'" (v. 3). Rachel proposed the same foolish course of action that Sarah had before her. In her loss of hope she would have done anything to ease the pain, up to and including things immoral or illegal.

Here we see the heart of God who, even in the face of disobedience, stupidity, and human failure, refused to be put off. He is and always was a God of grace. "Then God remembered Rachel, and God gave heed to her and opened her womb" (v. 22). The season of extended barrenness is the time of more fervent and consistent prayer. God heard her desperation. "So she conceived and bore a son and said, 'God has taken away my reproach'" (v. 23).

God honored the barren womb and put an end to torment and shame. "She named him Joseph, saying, 'May the LORD give me another son'" (v. 24). Joseph, child of the barren womb, grew up to stand beside Pharaoh at a strategic point in history and save his family—the line of Abraham, the nation of promise—from starvation.

THE STORY OF HANNAH

[Elkanah] had two wives: the name of one was Hannah and the name of the other Peninnah; and Peninnah had children, but Hannah had no children. Now this man would go up from his city yearly to worship and to sacrifice to the LORD of hosts in Shiloh. And the two sons of Eli, Hophni and Phinehas, were priests to the LORD there. When the day came that Elkanah sacrificed, he would give portions to Peninnah his wife and to all her sons and her daughters; but to Hannah he would give a double portion, for he loved Hannah, but the LORD had closed her womb.

—1 SAMUEL 1:2–5

"The Lord had closed her womb": it may seem hard to swallow, but the truth is that when the fruit seems held back, it is, indeed, the hand of God—who keeps His own counsel regarding timing and delay. Hannah's rival, however, "would provoke her bitterly to irritate her, because the LORD had closed her womb" (1 Sam. 1:6).

Once again, note that family conflict can arise in the wake of extended delay. One family member felt superior to the other, fell to jealousy of her husband's preference for her rival, and did all she could to torment her. "It happened year after year, as often as she went up to the house of the LORD, she would provoke her; so she wept and would not eat" (v. 7). Again: depression, broken hope, despair.

How many of us have looked around at what we think others have in the Lord and felt wounding or rejection because we feel they've been favored in ways we have not? In this case one wife suffered because she knew she wasn't loved, while the other despaired because the Lord had closed her womb. In different ways, each felt left out and rejected.

> Then Elkanah her husband said to her, "Hannah, why do you weep and why do you not eat and why is your heart sad? Am I not better to you than ten sons?" Then Hannah rose after eating and drinking in Shiloh. Now Eli the priest was sitting on the seat by the doorpost of the temple of the LORD. She, greatly distressed, prayed to the LORD and wept bitterly.
> —1 SAMUEL 1:8–10

The season of long deferred hope became the time of desperate, broken, and humble prayer:

> She made a vow and said, "O Lord of hosts, if You will indeed look on the affliction of Your maidservant and remember me, and not forget Your maidservant, but will give Your maidservant a son, then I will give him to the Lord all the days of his life, and a razor shall never come on his head."
>
> —1 Samuel 1:11

In that verse lies an important key to ultimate fulfillment of the promise and realization of hope long delayed. Who is it all for? Is it really about you? Or would you surrender it to the Lord and refuse to selfishly own it? Would it truly be for Him and for the kingdom of God?

God called Abraham to sacrifice Isaac, his only son, the son of promise, and his obedience qualified him to father the nation. Generations later Hannah chose not to own the child of promise as her own and sacrificed him to God before the child would even be conceived. The Lord may refuse to open the womb of your life until you are ready to sacrifice it all to Him so that the fulfillment will be about the kingdom of God, not you:

> Now it came about, as she continued praying before the Lord, that Eli was watching her mouth. As for Hannah, she was speaking in her heart, only her lips were moving, but her voice was not heard. So Eli thought she was drunk. Then Eli

said to her, "How long will you make yourself drunk? Put away your wine from you."

—1 SAMUEL 1:12–14

That passage presents us with yet another key: it may be important to honor and respect even the dishonorable and insensitive priest or Christian leader. In our culture if a pastor misses it, makes an insensitive statement, or commits some other kind of wrong, we tend to run off to another church and tell everyone how that pastor was so abusive. Listen, however, to Hannah's response of respect for the position Eli held:

> But Hannah replied, "No, my lord, I am a woman oppressed in spirit; I have drunk neither wine nor strong drink, but I have poured out my soul before the LORD. Do not consider *your maidservant* as a worthless woman, for I have spoken until now out of my great concern and provocation." Then Eli answered and said, "Go in peace; and may the God of Israel grant your petition that you have asked of Him."
>
> —1 SAMUEL 1:15–17, EMPHASIS ADDED

The honor she gave in the face of Eli's insensitivity released a blessing through the priest in the position of authority. She could very well have reacted in hurt and bitterness, but she chose not to.

Some of us have remained barren in our lives, mired in disappointment and frustration, because we've never been able to absorb this lesson about giving honor. The culture in which we live cultivates dishonor toward authority, and now we reap the destruction culture-wide.

She said, "Let your maidservant find favor in your sight." So the woman went her way and ate, and her face was no longer sad. Then they arose early in the morning and worshiped before the LORD, and returned again to their house in Ramah. And Elkanah had relations with Hannah his wife, and the LORD remembered her. It came about in due time, after Hannah had conceived, that she gave birth to a son; and she named him Samuel, saying, "Because I have asked him of the LORD."

—1 SAMUEL 1:18–20

Hannah kept her word and in due time surrendered Samuel to the Lord, giving him into Eli's hands to care for and train. Samuel became yet another key player in redemptive history, born of a barren woman, anointing kings and exercising the raw power and authority of God.

THE FRUIT OF FAITHFULNESS

In the days of Herod, king of Judea, there was a priest named Zacharias, of the division of Abijah; and he had a wife from the daughters of Aaron, and her name was Elizabeth.

—LUKE 1:5

On the surface you would think this couple highly blessed. A marriage in which both the man and the woman could trace their heritage through the priestly line was considered a double blessing, but they faced a serious difficulty that called the blessing into question.

As is the case with so many of us today, there seemed to be no discernable reason for the blessing to be withheld. "They were both righteous in the sight of God, walking blamelessly in all the commandments and requirements of the Lord" (Luke 1:6). Heartbreak dominated their lives, but despite this, they stood by the Lord in solid faithfulness year after year. In the face of deferred hope, how many of us would fall into a pity party and simply quit? To reap the blessing of seeing the barren womb of your life opened, however, you must be in position to receive it when it happens, no matter what you feel. That is the fruit of faithfulness.

"But they had no child, because Elizabeth was barren, and they were both advanced in years" (v. 7). As far as Zacharias and Elizabeth knew, it was over for them. For Elizabeth, this meant disgrace as a woman and ongoing shame and despair. How many times over the years had her menstrual period come late and their hopes risen, only to be dashed again?

As a priest, Zacharias was part of a division that would serve the temple two weeks out of the year. During that time one of their number would be chosen by lot to enter the holy of holies to burn incense to the Lord in prayer. That year the lot fell to Zacharias, and while he was inside, the Lord turned his life upside down. An angel appeared to him, announcing Elizabeth would bear a son and that this son, born of a barren womb, would play a key role in redemptive history:

> For he will be great in the sight of the Lord; and he will drink no wine or liquor, and he will be filled with the Holy Spirit while yet in his mother's womb. And he will turn many of the sons of Israel back to the Lord their God. It is he who will

go as a forerunner before Him in the spirit and power of Elijah, to turn the hearts of the fathers back to the children, and the disobedient to the attitude of the righteous, so as to make ready a people prepared for the Lord.

—LUKE 1:15–17

Their son, John the Baptist, represented the restoration of prophecy after four hundred years of silence and would prepare the way for Jesus. He would become a key figure in redemptive history, born of a barren and fruitless womb at an impossible point in the lives of Zacharias and Elizabeth.

"Zacharias said to the angel, 'How will I know this for certain? For I am an old man and my wife is advanced in years'" (Luke 1:18). Deep into a lifetime of despair due to hope deferred, Zacharias couldn't believe the promise, even in the face of an angelic visitation. Here we see again a loss of faith resulting from the heartbreak of the barren womb. I suspect that, as a way to cope with the pain, Zacharias had made peace with a settled unbelief and loss of hope. All he had left was his faithfulness and service to the Lord.

For his part, the angel now erupted in anger! "The angel answered and said to him, 'I am Gabriel, who stands in the presence of God, and I have been sent to speak to you and to bring you this good news. And behold, you shall be silent and unable to speak until the day when these things take place, because you did not believe my words, which will be fulfilled in their proper time'" (vv. 19–20).

Unbelief comes at a price, but your emotional unbelief

will never be great enough to turn aside the promise unless you become unfaithful, out of position to receive the promise when it comes. Faithfulness is a vital key to fulfillment of hope and promise.

The Lord kept His word and Elizabeth conceived. "This is the way the Lord has dealt with me in the days when He looked with favor upon me, to take away my disgrace among men" (v. 25). The heartache of disgrace and her sense of worthlessness vanished in the joy of hope fulfilled.

WAIT FOR THE PROMISE

Many of us know all too well the agony of the barren womb represented in the unfulfilled promises for which we have waited so long. It seems our lives have produced little next to the promises we have received and compared with the hopes and dreams birthed in our hearts.

At this writing, in light of the anointing the Lord has given us and the quality of what we offer, the congregation I pastor should be five times its current size, if prophetic words spoken by the best servants the Lord has to offer had come to pass. I know firsthand, therefore, the heartache, the erosion of hope, the conflict, and even the judgments that can be leveled from those who just don't get it but who think they're so holy. Sooner or later barrenness draws reproach and shame.

For a very long time, however, God has been bringing about key turnings in the redemptive history of His people through the barren wombs of hopeless and discounted servants. He's still doing it. He'll do it for you. First, *remember that God is faithful to His promise,* even if it takes a long time. Second, *stand your ground in faithfulness* and don't let go, no matter how long it takes. Third, *pray desperately and consistently* in humility.

God calls history makers out of the barren places and the vastness of the wilderness. Those are the places where godly people get their training.

Wait for it: the promise is coming!

Chapter 9

THE DISAPPOINTMENT OF
DELAYED PROMISES

———◆———

T wo of the most significant prophetic books of the Old Testament are Isaiah and Jeremiah. Both of the men who wrote them prophesied to apostate Israel, declaring that Judah and Jerusalem would be destroyed and the people exiled from their homeland. Israel's sins were heinous, including both temple prostitution and child sacrifice. Far from being pronouncements of a judgmental and angry God, the words Isaiah and Jeremiah spoke were those of a loving and patient Father driven to extreme measures for the sake of His people after centuries of pleading for repentance.

The psalmist wrote that the angel of the Lord encamps around those who fear Him and rescues them (Ps. 34:7). Protected and blessed, the people of God prosper. Israel protested that they believed in the Lord, but their behavior and their inclusion of other gods in their worship revealed the truth about their lack of real fear and respect for Him.

What you believe isn't what you think in your head. It's what you do. Therefore, not only did the angel of the Lord no longer shield them and ensure blessing for them, but also, as a last resort to restore them to Himself, God raised up an enemy against them who would destroy their nation and carry them into exile.

Seventy Years of Exile

The exile would last seventy years before the people would be permitted to return to their ancestral home. God, however, made glorious promises to them beforehand for their restoration and to plant hope for the final outcome:

> O afflicted one, storm-tossed, and not comforted, behold, I will set your stones in antimony, and your foundations I will lay in sapphires. Moreover, I will make your battlements of rubies, and your gates of crystal, and your entire wall of precious stones. All your sons will be taught of the Lord; and the well-being of your sons will be great. In righteousness you will be established; you will be far from oppression, for you will not fear; and from terror, for it will not come near you. If anyone fiercely assails you it will not be from Me. Whoever assails you will fall because of you.
> —Isaiah 54:11–15

> For thus says the Lord, "When seventy years have been completed for Babylon, I will visit you and fulfill My good word to you, to bring you back to this place. For I know the plans that I have for you," declares the Lord, "plans for welfare and

not for calamity to give you a future and a hope.
Then you will call upon Me and come and pray to
Me, and I will listen to you. You will seek Me and
find Me when you search for Me with all your
heart. I will be found by you," declares the LORD,
"and I will restore your fortunes and will gather
you from all the nations and from all the places
where I have driven you," declares the LORD,
"and I will bring you back to the place from where
I sent you into exile."

—JEREMIAH 29:10–14

For those seventy long years Jerusalem lay in a heap
of rubble, the walls broken down and the temple of
the Lord destroyed. Covered in weeds and inhabited
by wild animals, the land languished. As the time for
fulfilling the promises approached, seven decades had
passed, and scarcely anyone remained from the generation who had seen the land in its former glory. A
few of the very old remembered, but most of the people
were so young that they knew only secondhand stories
of the glory days, the beauty of the temple, and the
richness of the land—their elders' distant memories of
another time.

Although prophetic promises of restoration had been
spoken to the people, the fulfillment must have felt to
them like delay and then more delay. When the nation
left Egypt under Moses, the wilderness sojourn lasted
only forty years, but this exile had stretched through
nearly two generations.

The Pain of Delay

When promises seem to be delayed, and then delayed again, your heart hurts, and eventually the pain opens into a bleeding wound as disappointment mounts. In an effort to mitigate the pain of repeated letdowns, you tend to stop believing in the promises. As hope erodes, you might even give up altogether. If allowed to, hurt can make you self-centered—and that's when you really begin to suffer loss.

Put in simple terms, when you stub your bare toe on a concrete step, you're not thinking about anyone but yourself and how you want to kill the fool who built the step that way. If you allow it, pain can make you self-centered!

Years ago I had surgery to remove six inches of my colon. Lying in the hospital in a world of hurt, I found myself muttering, "I want my Reah" (my youngest daughter), over and over again. It wasn't that I had a prophetic word for her or that I wanted to bless her. I wasn't thinking about her welfare at all. In my pain I wanted someone I loved near me to make me feel better, and I didn't much care what might going on in her life at the time. Pain does that to you.

There's really nothing wrong with self-focus in that context, but emotional pain and lost hope aren't nearly as innocuous in their effect on us. They can make you self-centered in all the wrong ways and can ultimately disconnect you from God. They can throw water on the fire of your love for people and for the Lord. In that state of being, life becomes all about you and what you personally feel. You can lose touch with others and their needs without even understanding how you got there. You can even forget your connection with God.

An emotionally self-centered group of Judeans therefore returned home from exile—a people whose hope had been broken for almost two generations, but now revived with expectation of a better day. With at least a measure of the promise of restoring old glory, fueled by old memories passed on by their elders and the prophecies of Isaiah and Jeremiah, they came to their long-lost homeland.

Even in the face of the beginning of fulfillment, they almost didn't believe it. I've experienced this personally. Once hope has been shattered, picking it up again can be difficult, even when the reality of the promise begins to unfold. The promise may have been huge, but the beginning of fulfillment almost always will be small and fraught with difficulty.

Self-focused pain, therefore, can prevent you from buying in just at the time when it would be vital that you do so. Fear of being let down once more can bring on paralysis. The thought is, if you allow yourself to hope yet once more, then you can be wounded more deeply than you already have been, if the promise fails to materialize.

In that wounding you can become even more wrapped up in yourself than you were before. And when you get more wrapped up in yourself, you become more blind to what God is actually doing. This renders you incapable of investing in the promise at the level of intensity needed to build on it and inherit the blessing.

With some measure of heightened expectation, then,

the people of Israel returned to their ancestral home to find a devastated land.

A DISAPPOINTING RETURN

Just after the Iron Curtain came down in Europe, my wife and I ministered in East Germany. Crossing the old border between East and West, we were shocked at the contrast. Although several decades had passed, portions of the eastern segment of the country looked as if the bombs had fallen just yesterday. Where the Allied firebombing during World War II had destroyed the cultural heart of Dresden, the city remained a jumbled wasteland of tumbled stones that had been buildings. Weeds grew up in the spaces between. This is what Israel saw when they returned to the land—as if the devastation had all happened just the day before.

The temple lay in rubble. Once verdant fields were given to weeds and wild grass. Because grape vines take time and attention to make them produce, any that may have remained alive had long since gone wild. To add to the people's problems, they had no place to live. I imagine that as they took all this in, absorbing the deeper pain of lost hope revived and then dashed again, they were thinking: "Where's the glory? This doesn't look like the promises we heard from those prophets or what we've waited so long to see! And we left the richness of Babylon behind for *this*?"

Nevertheless, they went to work building homes and planting fields, trying hard to make a life, but nothing they did seemed to work. In the face of their disappointment they allowed themselves to turn inward:

> In the second year of Darius the king, on the first
> day of the sixth month, the word of the LORD
> came by the prophet Haggai to Zerubbabel the son
> of Shealtiel, governor of Judah, and to Joshua the
> son of Jehozadak, the high priest, saying, "Thus
> says the Lord of hosts, 'This people says, "The time
> has not come, even the time for the house of the
> LORD to be rebuilt."'"
>
> —HAGGAI 1:1–2

They said this because they had become completely
absorbed in securing their own lives before they would
invest in the kingdom of God. Personal and individual
prosperity became their priority in the face of hope
deferred. What they were saying, in effect, was, "The
temple, the things of God, can wait until we think we
can afford it, until we've taken care of ourselves." But
nothing was working as they wanted it to:

> Then the word of the LORD came by Haggai the
> prophet, saying, "Is it time for you yourselves to
> dwell in your paneled houses while this house lies
> desolate?" Now therefore, thus says the LORD of
> hosts, "Consider your ways! You have sown much,
> but harvest little; you eat, but there is not enough
> to be satisfied; you drink, but there is not enough
> to become drunk; you put on clothing, but no
> one is warm enough; and he who earns, earns
> wages to put into a purse with holes."
>
> —HAGGAI 1:3–6

Everything they tried seemed to be blocked. They
worked hard, but for little return, and everything leaked
away that appeared as if it might produce increase.

Their economy had stalled, and they wanted to know why. God answered:

> Thus says the LORD of hosts, "Consider your ways! Go up to the mountains, bring wood and rebuild the temple, that I may be pleased with it and be glorified," says the LORD. "You look for much, but behold, it comes to little; when you bring it home, I blow it away. Why?" declares the LORD of hosts, "Because of My house which lies desolate, while each of you runs to his own house. Therefore, because of you the sky has withheld its dew and the earth has withheld its produce. I called for a drought on the land, on the mountains, on the grain, on the new wine, on the oil, on what the ground produces, on men, on cattle, and on all the labor of your hands."
>
> —HAGGAI 1:7–11

None of that had come about by chance. It strikes me that God *Himself* blew it all away. God Himself stood against them. God Himself would not allow them to prosper because the self-centered mind-set that had developed in them over seventy years of hope deferred, together with the impact of the devastated condition of the land, had caused them to flip their priorities. The new order of importance was: "Me first, and the kingdom of God can wait. I'll give what's left over when I'm done with me."

THE TEMPLE AND THE KINGDOM OF GOD

Was God really that concerned with a building? Not really. His concern was for what the building stood for. For God, the temple was a huge issue because in Bible times it was seen as the physical dwelling place of God. It contained the holy of holies, the very throne room of God that symbolized His authority and rule. It stood for the dedication of the people to their God and formed the physical center of their lives in Him.

That made it the top priority. To neglect the temple was to deny the sovereignty and position of God as the center of their lives. Isn't it true that when times grow difficult and hearts begin to hurt, the first thing Christians today hold back is their giving?

In the New Testament we the people constitute the temple. We become the dwelling place of God as the Holy Spirit fills our life together. In our relationships with one another and with the Lord we form a visible structure that declares the authority and glory of the Lord:

> So then you are no longer strangers and aliens, but you are fellow citizens with the saints, and are of God's household, having been built on the foundation of the apostles and prophets, Christ Jesus Himself being the corner stone, in whom the whole building, being fitted together, is growing into a holy temple in the Lord, in whom you also are being built together into a dwelling of God in the Spirit.
> —EPHESIANS 2:19–22

The Old Testament temple made a visible statement of what the people believed and knew about the glory of God. In the New Testament, that would remain true to some extent. Outsiders draw conclusions concerning what we think of God by looking at the physical buildings in which we worship. But the point is that for us, whether it's the physical facility or the temple of our oneness as a people, the temple symbolizes kingdom things. It makes a public statement about who God is in His sovereignty, His love, His power, and His miracles.

In the relationships that bind us together, the temple of living stones declares the love He pours out for us. The temple is the building in which we become together as a people; in our oneness, making a statement to the world about who God is by the way we live, give, minister, and share.

So the principle continues to apply. Commitment to the building of the temple, creating that visible statement and living selflessly for the sake of the kingdom of God, must take priority over our personal financial and material well-being. If that priority is out of whack, the principle remains that nothing works: "'You look for much, but behold, it comes to little; when you bring it home, I blow it away. Why?' declares the LORD of hosts, 'Because of My house which lies desolate, while each of you runs to his own house'" (Hag. 1:9). Conversely, when that principle is in order, the blessing of God flows.

It's all too easy to skew your focus and do all the wrong things when fear takes hold and you allow delayed promises to become a sickness and a cancer of the soul. Matters then become worse. "Hope deferred makes the heart sick, but desire fulfilled is a tree of life" (Prov. 13:12).

SETTING KINGDOM PRIORITIES

Some of the first verses anyone learns in Sunday school are Matthew 6:31–33: "Do not worry then, saying, 'What will we eat?' or 'What will we drink?' or 'What will we wear for clothing?' For the Gentiles eagerly seek all these things; for your heavenly Father knows that you need all these things. But seek first His kingdom and His righteousness, and all these things will be added to you." In Haggai's day the temple was only a visible representation of the kingdom of God, a place to focus the priority.

I was a stupid kid before I became a less-than-wise adult. I had a father who tried again and again to save me from my own stupidity. Most of the time I wouldn't listen. He told me not to jump off high places using an umbrella for a parachute. He told me this, not because he was a legalist laying the law on me—and certainly not because he was some kind of killjoy trying to limit my fun. He told me not to jump off high places using an umbrella for a parachute because he loved me and did not want me to hurt myself. He knew how reality actually works, and I didn't. Of course I did it anyway, and when it didn't work the first time, I did it some more until I hurt so badly I had to stop.

Neither did Haggai lay legalism on the people in calling for a temple priority, any more than Jesus spoke legalism when He called for a primary focus on seeking the kingdom. What Haggai and Jesus had to say was simply this: "Before you jump off the high place, get a parachute because the umbrella won't work. If you choose the umbrella instead, then don't blame God when you break an ankle or think that He somehow let you down. He didn't. Seek first the kingdom of God. It can't work any other way. It will never work any other way." Dedication to the building of the temple was simply a practical way of putting the kingdom of God first.

When God says these things to us and calls us to seek the kingdom first, it's relational, spiritual, and material. What does the kingdom of God mean for my relationships? My spiritual life? My material goods? In Malachi 3, for instance, the reason for the tithe, or the 10 percent of income, isn't so we can get rich. Neither is avoiding the curse meant to be the motivating factor. Tithing is not the magic button that, if you push it, everything is supposed to be easy. Yes, when an entire people neglect the tithe, God does call it theft, and the prosperity level of the people declines. But the primary reason for the tithe is this: "Bring the whole tithe into the storehouse, so that there may be food in My house" (Mal. 3:10).

That's relational. That's kingdom business. It's a love priority. God claims the tithe as His own so that the temple of the Lord can serve as a place of mercy ministry, feeding the poor, clothing the naked, and healing lives. Tithing as a discipline is a building block for overcoming self-focus for the sake of the kingdom and those who benefit from it.

The bonus is:

> "Test Me now in this," says the LORD of hosts, "if I will not open for you the windows of heaven and pour out for you a blessing until it overflows. Then I will rebuke the devourer for you, so that it will not destroy the fruits of the ground; nor

will your vine in the field cast its grapes," says the LORD of hosts. "All the nations will call you blessed, for you shall be a delightful land."

—MALACHI 3:10–12

That's not law. That's blessing. It points to self-sacrificial relationship and love. It's saying: "If you will love in concrete, sacrificial, and practical ways, even with material wealth, I will rebuke the devourer for you." According to Jesus's words in Matthew 6:33, that principle is neither law nor legalism. It's just God's love telling us how the universe works.

Those people, however, who had returned to the land after long years of exile were stuck, trapped in a depressive mind-set of hope deferred. Hurt and fear had made them self-centered and had focused them on their own prosperity at the expense of the kingdom of God—and it wasn't working. It never does because it can't.

You will never fly no matter how hard you flap your arms. Umbrellas will never be parachutes. Never will you breathe like a fish no matter how much you love the water. The fact that we're under grace and not law doesn't change any of that. It's just reality. This is the principle I'm articulating. Do you believe the Bible? Is it the truth? If you believe it, then you do it by covenant, not by feeling or mood. If you don't do it, then you don't believe it. Show me what you do, or don't do, and I'll show you what you truly believe regardless of your words.

What mind-set do most of us live under, and if it needs changing, how do we do that? Is it a mind-set that puts the kingdom of God first and demonstrates that priority first, not just with feelings but with actions and material sacrifice? Or is it a mind-set stuck in a heart made sick and self-centered by deferred hope, fear, stress, or unbelief?

CHANGING THE MIND-SET

How do you change a mind-set? How do you develop a renewed mind that moves in faith and not in fear? How do you renew hope when hope has died so that you don't miss out on what God is doing? How do you turn emotional self-centeredness that results in material self-centeredness into an attitude of hope and victory? How do you restore what has been lost and overcome the burden of disappointment?

Haggai prophesied the answer. Faith and renewal develop when we take concrete actions in the face of fear and disappointment. We overcome evil by choosing a corresponding good. Romans 12:21 illustrates this: "Do not be overcome by evil, but overcome evil with good." That verse, in context, applies to responding to an enemy, but it also expresses a general principle for overcoming attitudes of the heart that fail to reflect the goodness of Jesus and the promise of God. Overcome the curse by choosing to bless. Overcome self-absorption by choosing to give. Overcome fear by doing the righteous thing you fear to do—or that depression tells you *not* to do.

THE END OF THE STORY

Then Zerubbabel the son of Shealtiel, and Joshua the son of Jehozadak, the high priest, with all the

remnant of the people, obeyed the voice of the
LORD their God and the words of Haggai the
prophet, as the LORD their God had sent him.
And the people showed reverence for the LORD.

—HAGGAI 1:12

There's the key. Set a priority on showing reverence
for the Lord—not after your life is settled and secure or
because your life is settled and secure, but in order to
settle and secure your life. Overcome the disappointment of deferred promise by investing in the promise, no
matter how small or insecure the beginning may seem.

This cannot be a mere emotional thing, as if you were
waiting for the right feeling before making it happen.
This must be practical and material, a decision pursued
on the basis of covenant commitment. As James wrote,
"Even so faith, if it has no works, is dead, being by itself.
But someone may well say, 'You have faith and I have
works; show me your faith without the works, and I will
show you my faith by my works'" (James 2:17–18). What
we actually do, or don't do, reveals what we believe and
what we are truly dedicated to.

The returning exiles took Haggai's words to heart
and changed their priorities. According to the promise
of God, fruit resulted:

As for the promise which I made you when you
came out of Egypt, My Spirit is abiding in your
midst; do not fear! For thus says the LORD of hosts,
"Once more in a little while, I am going to shake
the heavens and the earth, the sea also and the
dry land. I will shake all the nations; and they will
come with the wealth of all nations, and I will fill

this house with glory," says the LORD of hosts. "The silver is Mine and the gold is Mine," declares the LORD of hosts. "The latter glory of this house will be greater than the former," says the LORD of hosts, "and in this place I will give peace," declares the LORD of hosts.

—HAGGAI 2:5–9

A VISION OF RELEASE

In 2011, as I sat at a conference waiting to speak, I was suddenly impressed by a mental image of two parallel chains set vertically over a golden coin. Rarely am I given revelation by means of vision or mental picture, so I paid attention and began to seek the meaning of what I saw.

Clearly this image represented financial wealth and abundance that have been held back. Along with the rest of the world, we believers have suffered financially in recent years. As a nation and as a world we have undergone the Lord's judgment, and the church has not been exempt.

It has not, however, been God's judgment in the form of punishment or wrath. It has rather been *krisis*—a Greek New Testament word for "judgment" that means "to cut or separate." It has been judgment that is sent by God, even welcomed by His people, as that which separates the precious from the vile, what is holy from what is unholy and what is godly from what is ungodly. Promised financial abundance and release have been held back, and it has been instead a time of refining and purifying for those who have been able to receive it as such.

For many of us believers, these years of trial and delayed promise have been a purifying fire in which we have been forced to adjust and establish our priorities and commitments while our faithfulness has been put to the test. In 2006 I prophesied to the people of my church the recession that began in 2008. I told them we would be tested and that we would soon discover where our real faith rested—in material well-being or in the Lord, our true provider. I told them that we as a congregation would be preserved through the difficult times to come.

God has kept His word to us. Unlike many other churches, we did not have to cut back on programs or lay off staff. In fact, we expanded our outreaches to the poor, to Native American reservations, and to missions in Eastern Europe. Households have been stressed but preserved.

We and many others in other parts of the body of Christ have stood our ground and embraced the refining fire of judgment—*krisis*—in a way that has purified our devotion to God and confirmed our obedience to Him. I believe that the release of the gold coin from the restraining chains may now be imminent. The time has come for the Lord's justice to be realized—for the breaking of those chains and the release of provision for the kingdom of God that has been held back. The key to that release is and always has been a heart of sacrificial and faithful giving. Speaking of the righteous in Psalm 112, Scripture says in verse 3, "Wealth and riches are in his house, and his righteousness endures forever"; and in the fifth verse, "It is well with the man who is gracious and lends; he will maintain his cause in judgment."

I believe that the faithful, both individuals and ministries, will be miraculously blessed in days to come with financial provision even as the world around us suffers. Generosity has always been key to the release of God's provision and wealth. Jesus promised that if we sow, then we must reap (Luke 6:38). He who sows little reaps little, and he who fails to sow anything at all reaps nothing at all. This is not magic or self-centered manipulation of God's principles; rather, it is a function of the kingdom of God in line with the idea that love begets more love and grace begets greater grace. We give, not to get, but because it is right to give and because giving is an expression of love, whether or not we expect to reap a benefit.

SACRIFICE RELEASES POWER

It is also true that sacrifice releases power. Witness the power that fell on Solomon's temple when the priests offered up thousands of animals in sacrifice. The glory cloud filled the temple, and the priests couldn't stand up to minister (1 Kings 8:1–11). Witness the power released upon all of us when Jesus became our sacrifice for sin offered once for all.

I know, therefore, that in these days to come we must not measure our giving to fit our fear of not having enough for ourselves; rather, we must give in a way that constitutes sacrifice. If we wait to give until we feel that we can, we will never get there. If we give only when we feel we have enough to give, then giving is no longer a sacrifice. Sacrifice costs something. It involves risk.

What I'm really saying is that we must not walk in fear in the days to come, adjusting our generosity to fit either our fears or our loss of hope due to deferred fulfillment of God's promises. To do so would mean seeing the release of blessing continue being chained up. We must be generous as the heart of God is generous, no matter how we feel. The people of the church in Acts 2 had little materially, yet they sacrificially sold their property and possessions to meet the needs of others and then reaped the glory in signs, wonders, amazing love, and thousands of salvations.

The world may descend into economic chaos. Times of uncertainty may be extended indefinitely. Promises may be delayed, but I believe we who stand for truth are being offered a release of blessing spiritually, relationally, and, yes, economically so that we might have the resources available to minister richly to a dying world. Ministering to those who need is the greatest lift I know for a heart sick from deferred hope.

Chapter 10

A NEW EXPERIENCE OF WORSHIP

———◆———

T he first calling and task of the church and its people is to worship God. While the world can duplicate everything else we do, worship stands alone as the one activity in which the world cannot successfully engage. If they try, the effort produces a counterfeit.

We can heal people, but the world outside has its versions of healing. There's nothing like good Christian fellowship, but fellowship can be found on the golf course, on softball teams, at the Elks Lodge, at an Alcoholics Anonymous meeting, or at the local bar or club. Jesus calls us to care for the poor, feed the hungry, and clothe the naked, but these things can be done by organizations and agencies having no religious affiliation at all. Though we offer counseling guided and inspired by the Holy Spirit, the world provides counseling as well. Churches may sponsor Christian schools to educate children, but the world engages in education on a massive scale.

As God's people, we should be doing all these things and infusing them with our spirituality—but the one thing we do uniquely is to worship God. No one else can offer that.

This makes worship our first priority above all other forms of endeavor. After Moses led the Israelites out of Egypt, the first thing he did was to ascend Mount Sinai to receive the Law. The Law begins with the Ten Commandments because, for worship to be pure and undefiled, character and morality must be established. God then gave directions for building the tabernacle—the big tent constructed as a mobile place of worship—and with it came detailed instructions for how to conduct worship under its covering. Worship became the center of Israel's national life, a primary activity taking precedence over all else.

Because they understood the importance of the tabernacle, the people gave sacrificially from their own possessions to build that mobile temple and institute worship in it. They contributed gifts of gold and silver—the first and best of all they owned, including personal jewelry—to be melted down to make utensils for the sacrifices. Wooden furnishings were covered in gold overlay.

For God's honor, only the best would do. From the very moment the Lord called a people to be His own, worship stood as the top priority and a first calling: "You shall love the LORD your God with all your heart and with all your soul and with all your might" (Deut. 6:5).

Tabernacle sacrifices had to be the first and best of the people's animals as well as the first and best of their material goods. They knew that only the best would truly please God and honor Him. Songs and instrumental music were included, but worship centered on sacrifice and offerings.

God hasn't changed. He remains the same yesterday, today, and forever (Heb. 13:8). Our primary calling as His people, therefore, remains unchanged. Worship stands eternal as the first priority, the goal of which is still to bless God for His own sake. I want—as do many of you reading this book—for worship to be all it can be. We long for the genuine presence of God. I believe this must begin with an adjustment of focus.

THE FOCUS OF OUR WORSHIP

Other faiths worship their various gods, so what makes our worship different? How was Israel's worship to be differentiated from the worship of Baal, Molech, or any of the other gods of the day? As fertility gods, Baal and Molech were believed to ensure prosperity in return for the offerings and sacrifices of the people. Baal would cause worshippers' crops to grow and their herds to increase. Worship of Baal and Molech, therefore, catered to and fed self-focus.

Unlike the self-orientation of the nations around them, Israel's worship was intended to please the heart of God for God's own sake. At least, that was how it was supposed to be. When our worship becomes an entertainment event pandering to the needs of the people with the goal of hyping them into some form of excitement for their own pleasure, we've lost our way. When it becomes something we pursue as a way to get something from it for ourselves, we've lost our way.

When we lose sight of blessing God for His sake, we have reverted to the worship of Baal, and it's all downhill from there. It has become idolatry by another name.

Unfortunately this is what contemporary worship has become in some places—certainly not in all—and is one reason many of us find ourselves disappointed.

As the center point of the life of God's people from the time of Moses until now, worship opens the windows of heaven and connects us with God. It empowers and shapes the flavor of everything we do. When we offer up selfless worship, our labor in every other area of ministry will become selfless as well. Because God empowers what pleases Him, then by extension empowered worship energizes every other endeavor. Worship of God for God's sake brings the glory:

> And King Solomon and all the congregation of Israel, who were assembled to him, were with him before the ark, sacrificing so many sheep and oxen they could not be counted or numbered...It happened that when the priests came from the holy place, the cloud filled the house of the LORD, so that the priests could not stand to minister because of the cloud, for the glory of the LORD filled the house of the LORD.
>
> —1 KINGS 8:5, 10–11

Imagine glory so intense that it buckles the knees of the ministers of the Lord! I've been present on a number of occasions when this has happened!

IN SPIRIT AND TRUTH

Centuries later Jesus started a conversation with a disreputable Samaritan woman in a very public place, and the topic of worship came up. I say "disreputable" because she came to the well alone in the heat of the day.

All the so-called nice women of the town would have come in the cool of the early morning. In that culture no man would speak in public with a woman, whether reputable or disreputable, if she was not his wife. Additionally, this was Samaria, a region most Jews studiously avoided, believing the Samaritans to be defiled because of their mixed-race origins.

At first the conversation bordered on argument. The Jews claimed that God could be properly worshipped only in Jerusalem, while Samaritans held that God could be worshipped on the high places as well. Obviously hoping therefore to ignite an argument with this Jew who should not be passing through Samaria, the woman brought up this difference of opinion and hurled it in Jesus's face. Jesus rendered the entire argument about "place" irrelevant by saying:

> But an hour is coming, and now is, when the true worshipers will worship the Father in spirit and truth; for such people the Father seeks to be His worshipers. God is spirit, and those who worship Him must worship in spirit and truth.
>
> —JOHN 4:23–24

How, therefore, do we worship in spirit and truth? Some say that if we believe the right things about God, Jesus, and the Holy Spirit, then somehow that makes us worshippers in spirit and truth. The answer, however, lies not in doctrine, method, or location, but in connection at the level of spirit. Yet even this requires an explanation.

Three Kinds of Worshippers

1. Spiritual self-pleasers

My father has always had a fondness for colorful metaphors, not a few of which have landed him in trouble with the religious set. I think I inherited that from him because I have the same tendency to shake people up from time to time. My father says that too much of the worship he has seen in the places where he has traveled to minister is little more than spiritual masturbation—people working themselves up to produce a self-centered experience, a spiritual self-pleasuring.

Trying hard to make something happen, they strive to generate excitement and the supernatural by their own effort because their goal is to have an experience. Because it is focused on self, such worship begins and ends in the flesh. Ultimately it's not much different from thousands of youth crowding the stage at a secular rock concert, jumping up and down with their hands in the air, caught up in the excitement of the moment being generated by the performance on stage and the press of the crowd.

The godless culture in which we live conditions us to this unless we choose to resist it, as increasing numbers of us are doing. Under the influence of the surrounding culture, we seek entertainment and various forms of excitement, and we engage in it for what we can get out of it for ourselves. You see this when worship leaders hype a crowd, working up excitement for excitement's sake, stirring up the flesh to produce something that outwardly looks like a move of God but really isn't. The flesh is good at that. You know that we've missed true worship at some level when you hear people saying things like, "I get so much out of worship," as if we did it for our own benefit.

True worship has never been about getting a personal blessing. It never focuses on the quest to get something from it. To be real and fully Christian at the level of spirit and truth, worship must be offered to please God for God's sake. Was it what *He* wanted? Was it about giving *Him* honor?

This describes the great divide between the worshippers of God and the worshippers of Baal in Bible times. Devotees made offerings to Baal in order to move Baal to make them rich and prosperous. Israel made offerings to God in order to atone for sin, to repair the breach of relationship that sin created, and to thank and bless Him for what He had already done for them and would yet do. At least, that is how it was supposed to work.

We must, therefore, ask ourselves a question: Are we Baal worshippers seeking something for ourselves while believing that we're worshipping God, or are we worshippers of God in spirit and truth? The answer lies in discovering whom we're really doing it for—us or Him.

Too many believers have less than satisfying sex lives in their marriages because they haven't yet figured out that it's not what they're trying to get that makes sex glorious, but what they're giving for the sake of the marriage partner. It's the same with worship. The glory falls when we're giving it up for God's sake and God's pleasure. How many of you men bought your wife lingerie for her birthday and wondered why she didn't swoon over it? Whom was that for? If that was for you, then you were taking, not giving. That gift was about you.

And if it was about you rather than her, then ultimately it was just another form of use and abuse! Where are you with God and worship? It's the same principle.

2. "Bored with it" worshippers

It's possible for boredom in worship to stem from another form of focus on self. In the first chapter of Malachi God poured out His broken heart in complaint while the priests to whom He spoke responded defensively:

> "A son honors his father, and a servant his master. Then if I am a father, where is My honor? And if I am a master, where is My respect?" says the LORD of hosts to you, O priests who despise My name. But you say, "How have we despised Your name?" You are presenting defiled food upon My altar. But you say, "How have we defiled You?" In that you say, "The table of the LORD is to be despised." But when you present the blind for sacrifice, is it not evil? And when you present the lame and sick, is it not evil? Why not offer it to your governor? Would he be pleased with you? Or would he receive you kindly?" says the LORD of hosts.
>
> —MALACHI 1:6–8

At the heart of Israelite worship lay animal sacrifice. For sacrifices to fully honor Him, God called for offerings of perfect animals that cost the people something out of their material wealth. The priests, however, offered defective animals that were worthless even in the marketplace. After they kept the best for themselves, they offered up leftovers to God that wounded

His tender heart. These verses reveal the broken and bleeding heart of a loving Father pleading with His children. "If I am a Father, where is My honor?"

As an earthly father, I know I would be hurt if my children forgot my birthday or brought me a cake they had picked up free of charge because it had passed its expiration date. I'm honored and blessed by the sacrifices they make for me. My daughter-in-law makes me special cookies for Christmas and sometimes for my birthday. They're so good I can't stop eating them. I'm honored because it's the first and the best of her time and effort.

My children put time and thought into comments they write on the cards that come with my gifts, and my heart melts. The gifts my family brings on my birthday don't come secondhand from the thrift store. They're new. For my sixty-first birthday they bought me a Starbucks gift card, a gift card for Dairy Queen, and gift certificates for Benihana restaurants because they know my likes! The first and the best!

Focused on themselves, Israel was giving Father God leftovers. They kept the best for themselves, and it wounded God's heart because He loved them, while they dishonored Him. Because the priests offered less than the best, less than passion, worship had become boring and devoid of glory because they were dishonoring a loving God whose heart suffered hurt.

Worship becomes glorious when God pours out His pleasure in response to a sacrifice of the best we have to offer for His sake:

> "But now will you not entreat God's favor, that
> He may be gracious to us? With such an offering
> on your part, will He receive any of you kindly?"
> says the LORD of hosts. "Oh that there were one
> among you who would shut the gates, that you
> might not uselessly kindle fire on My altar! I am
> not pleased with you," says the LORD of hosts,
> "nor will I accept an offering from you."
>
> —MALACHI 1:9–10

Paraphrased, the message was: "I'm not going to allow you to continue to dishonor Me in My own house. That would damage both you and Me." It would be a farce, a serious breach of relationship.

The excellence of the sacrifice offered in real worship full of passion makes God appear great before the nations of the world.

> "For from the rising of the sun even to its setting,
> My name will be great among the nations, and in
> every place incense is going to be offered to My
> name, and a grain offering that is pure; for My
> name will be great among the nations," says the
> LORD of hosts.
>
> —MALACHI 1:11

Some of the most effective evangelism happens in the excellence, fire, and passion of our worship. Why would the world care for our God when they see us so laid back about Him that we exhibit no passion? Why would they believe our claims when they see us giving Him leftovers after we've taken the best for ourselves? Here is the boredom that profanes:

"But you are profaning it, in that you say, 'The table of the Lord is defiled, and as for its fruit, its food is to be despised.' You also say, 'My, how tiresome it is!' And you disdainfully sniff at it," says the LORD of hosts, "and you bring what was taken by robbery and what is lame or sick; so you bring the offering! Should I receive that from your hand?" says the LORD.

—MALACHI 1:12–13

Worship becomes lifeless and boring when it's for us and not for Him, when we begin to offer less than passion because it's all about whether or not *He* blesses *us*.

If the life has gone out of worship for you, don't blame the music, the worship leader, or the sound system. Look to your own heart. Is worship for you or for Him? Is it for delighting and blessing Him, or it is for you so you can have an experience? Is it the best you have to offer for His sake, or is it your emotional and material leftovers? Is it about what He feels, or is it about the mood you're having at the moment? If your answer is the wrong one, then worship will be boring because God won't show up for it.

3. Worshippers in spirit and truth

According to Malachi, the answer to the original question, "What is it to worship in spirit and truth?", is that worship is a sacrifice to God of the first and the best we have to offer in order to bless Him for His sake. Shouldn't our worship be modeled as much as possible directly after the original template as revealed in heaven?

As I describe it, I will employ some romantic and

sexual metaphors. If you have trouble with that, then you probably need to read the Song of Solomon very carefully.

In Revelation 5:8–9 the four living creatures (possibly the seraphim mentioned in Isaiah 6:1–3) and twenty-four elders in heaven (angelic representations of the whole people of God, twelve patriarchs and twelve apostles) begin their worship by singing a new song to the Lord. As they sing a song of praise to God, there's a freshness, an element of ongoing new creation, in what they offer.

Over the years much has been said of the difference between praise and worship. People often equate rowdy, upbeat songs with praise. When the music turns mellower, they call it worship. To me this doesn't even come close to describing how the two differ. The difference between praise and worship has nothing to do with rowdy or mellow. Ultimately it has to do with being where Jesus is in spirit. What's His mood? How is it worship if He's dancing with joy and we're going all mellow? Or how is it worship if He's being meditative and quiet while we dance our hearts out?

Whether rowdy or mellow, think of praise as the compliment one lover gives to another lover: "You're beautiful. I love your eyes. You're a wonderful woman," or, "You're a good man. Thank you for being who you are." Compliments like this release positive energy into a relationship. They feed and strengthen love and respect, like throwing wood on a fire or like starting lovemaking with foreplay. Without foreplay and without taking the necessary time for it, sex can very quickly become boring. It can even be that one partner takes pleasure at the expense of the other. In order to build toward a satisfying mutual climax, the partners must take time to build one another up. The living creatures and the elders therefore begin with a song of praise. They affirm and bless who Jesus is, giving compliments to the One they love, and energy begins to be released:

> And they sang a new song, saying, "Worthy are You to take the book and to break its seals; for You were slain, and purchased for God with Your blood men from every tribe and tongue and people and nation. You have made them to be a kingdom and priests to our God; and they will reign upon the earth."
>
> —REVELATION 5:9–10

It begins with the few and then spreads to the many as it grows in intensity, volume, and passion. The whole thing crescendos as compliments rise to God and as those compliments and affirmations release and gather power:

> Then I looked, and I heard the voice of many angels around the throne and the living creatures and the elders; and the number of them was myriads of myriads, and thousands of thousands, saying with a loud voice, "Worthy is the Lamb that was slain to receive power and riches and wisdom and might and honor and glory and blessing."
>
> —REVELATION 5:11–12

Passion builds toward a climax, just as passion mounts in the foreplay portion of lovemaking, growing more and more compelling.

In praise, the created ones—you and me—remain in control, because in this heavenly picture praise is a creaturely activity directed to God that connects the created beings with Him. Praise is the beginning of sacrifice. Sacrifice releases power. Make it a great sacrifice, and great power is released. As power is released, more voices join the ever-increasing volume while the power grows yet greater:

> And every created thing which is in heaven and on the earth and under the earth and on the sea, and all things in them, I heard saying, "To Him who sits on the throne, and to the Lamb, be blessing and honor and glory and dominion forever and ever." And the four living creatures kept saying, "Amen." And the elders fell down and worshiped.
> —REVELATION 5:13–14

They didn't voluntarily *get* down. Rather, they *fell* down and worshipped, overcome.

Finally, through praise—by lifting up the sacrifice of compliments and thanksgiving for the sake of the one they love—they build enough energy into the relationship that the release of climax comes, just as it does in lovemaking when foreplay has been pursued to its end. At this point they no longer have the passion but the passion has them. They have been overcome. If during sex you fail to reach that pinnacle because you haven't been selfless enough to be in it for your partner's pleasure, then the whole thing will be a disappointment. That is as true of worship as it is of lovemaking.

Worship is therefore the breakthrough that follows the sacrifice of praise pursued to its end. It's when the power of heaven overcomes human initiative and control. In the same way that you lose control in lovemaking, in worship you cease to have the passion under control and the passion of heaven has you as you surrender to it. Human doing ceases, and heaven's hand takes over. How can that be boring?

Worship reaches its most powerful stage and returns the greatest blessing when it's selfless, when we offer it not for the sake of obtaining a blessing for ourselves but rather to bless God alone for His sake with the first and the best of what we have to offer. Worship begins with our decision to praise, and in that sense it is what we make it. It climaxes with what God makes it, as we lose ourselves in Him.

The offering of defiled sacrifices in Malachi's day gave evidence that worship had ceased to be an act of love toward the Father. This wounded His tender heart and explains why He wanted to shut the door and end it. By contrast, I can sense God's pleasure when we offer up worship with passion and freedom. True worshippers can feel His heart swell when we give Him the best we have to offer. Angels show up for that kind of worship:

> I looked, and I heard the voice of many angels around the throne and the living creatures and the elders; and the number of them was myriads of myriads, and thousands of thousands.
> —REVELATION 5:11

By God's grace there have been times in worship at my own church when we have clearly heard angels singing with us and at least one occasion when an angelic flute soloed for us.

I choose to believe that glorious worship, offered in holy passion, will draw the nations, as the Lord said in Malachi 1:11: "My name will be great among the nations, and in every place incense is going to be offered to My name, and a grain offering that is pure; for My name will be great among the nations."

A FINAL PIECE

One more piece needs to be added to this picture of deeper and renewed worship for the truly hungry:

> And I heard a voice from heaven, like the sound of many waters and like the sound of loud thunder, and the voice which I heard was like the sound of harpists playing on their harps. And they sang a new song before the throne and before the four living creatures and the elders; and no one could learn the song except the one hundred and forty-four thousand who had been purchased from the earth.
>
> —REVELATION 14:2–3

In these last days a new anointing has come and is coming to worship that can flow only from the hearts of fully committed, laid-down lovers of God. It begins in heaven and it manifests on Earth. It can be truly entered into, or learned, only by those wholly given to the Lord. According to Revelation, it springs from hearts that have been profoundly changed, from those who are becoming conformed to the image of the Son of God (Rom. 8:29). This worship resonates with the Spirit of Jesus and is led by those who understand that what they offer up is so much more than music.

According to Revelation, compromisers and the lukewarm cannot learn this "song" or fully enter into this worship because it can come only from those who have hungered after purity of devotion, moral integrity, and love. The multitude will sense the presence of God in it, and perhaps even be drawn to it like moths to a flame, but they will not be able to comprehend its depth or power unless they make the sacrifice the laid-down lovers of God have made.

This kind of worship produces signs, wonders, healings, and prophetic words as God moves in a sovereign way in the midst of it. He touches His children with healing power without the mediation of any human agent, just because we've come into His raw presence.

We have experienced seasons of this in worship at my own church as people were healed of a variety of ailments, so I know more is coming. We offer this worship not for ourselves, but as a sacrifice to bless a loving God. It takes us more deeply into His presence—past the entertainment orientation, beyond the "feed me" attitude—to a place where the heavens open and we find ourselves in the throne room of the King, where tears are dried and suffering is washed away.

Chapter 11

PRAYING LIKE SONS
AND DAUGHTERS

————◆————

Aren't you tired of the methods of prayer we've been taught that promise to bear fruit, as if we had to get the words just right for God to move? Have you found that words don't have all the power you were told they did? Doesn't trying to figure out what God needs to hear kind of wear you out?

Twenty-five years ago I served on the teaching team at my father's ministry, Elijah House. For a time I traveled the world teaching inner healing, a term we always hated. We prefer *transformation*. Inevitably, in every session, someone looking for a method asked how they should pray for this or that bitter root, stronghold, or emotional wound. My answer never varied. "Just talk to your Father about your brother or sister," I'd say.

He won't deny us because we didn't get the "formula" right. It's not magic. Spells only work on *Charmed*, the former TV series about three witches who needed to rhyme everything before power would flow. God isn't like that, yet somehow the idea that we must learn or study how to do what should come naturally persists, and has from time immemorial.

What Jesus Taught

Not long after Jesus had chosen His disciples and gathered them to Himself to walk with Him, they began to ask questions about their relationship with the Father. They had followed Jesus around for a while and watched Him lovingly minister to people, heard His teaching, and sensed things in Him they had never imagined—things so different from the religion of the Pharisees that dominated their culture. It drew them in and created a hunger to understand, much like the longing so many feel today in their disappointment with the religion they've absorbed.

Instead of the dead rules, regulations, and lifeless principles the Pharisees had taught them, the disciples sensed the ease of love and intimacy Jesus enjoyed with His Father. It called out to them, and they wanted it for themselves. They knew that the Jewish rabbis taught their disciples how to pray. As they sensed the freshness and the glory of Jesus's relationship with the Father, the disciples asked Jesus to do the same for them.

Many of us right now can sense the nearness of something fresh from God about to break forth. It's like smelling great food cooking in the kitchen and not really knowing what it is, but it sends out such an aroma that it fills us with longing and anticipation. We feel the pull of the Father's heart and the Father's promise, like the scent of a good doughnut shop wafting on the breeze in the morning, calling to us to come spend our last bit of change to get that doughnut and satisfy the longing.

The disciples had learned the prescribed prayers of Judaism recited by rote at three set times a day. It made for copious repetition—the words were always the same, carefully formulated, and formally stated. They knew the disciples of the rabbis learned these things from their teachers—these obligations, methods, and forms—and they expected the same from Jesus. They wanted a method, an approach. Knowing that Jesus walked a different path, they asked Him for a new teaching on how to pray.

"PRAY, THEN, IN THIS WAY..."

"How do we do that, Jesus? Teach us to pray like You do," they asked. Responding to their hunger, He prayed aloud so that they could listen, hear, and learn. "Pray, then, in this way," He said (Matt. 6:9). The last thing He intended was that they would pray those specific words or turn the form into a method. He certainly didn't mean that they should repeat His prayer over and over again by rote.

Please understand that I'm not negating the value of memorizing the Lord's Prayer. It's one I love to say and sing. I'm only saying that in telling them to pray "in this way," Jesus meant for them to sense the spirit of it and catch the depth of relationship with the Father embedded in it.

Many of us have been longing for greater miracles; we long to see people we love healed and delivered from diseases, marriages restored, and relationships with children put back together. We want depression to be broken and hope to be fully released. We want to walk in joy ourselves and others to walk there too. We long for more visible demonstrations of His power and for more accurate and effective prophetic ministry. Our hearts cry to Him for souls to be saved and for everything God has promised to come to pass in our midst. Wouldn't it be great if we could just learn and recite all the right words and formulas that would compel God to act? Well, not really.

We know the answers don't lie in a method or approach we learned in a class or at a conference. We know we won't find it in those few gifted, superstar people we set up to do it all for us. What we really long for is deep intimacy with Father God. Jesus, therefore, didn't tell them, "Adopt this *method* of prayer," or "Follow this *model.*" He didn't give them five steps to a powerful prayer life or outline a teaching on "Prayers That Work," as if God were some puzzle to be solved before He could be moved to act on our behalf.

He taught them to pray "in this *way*" (emphasis added), to sense the heart of it. He wanted His disciples to have a relationship with Father God that reflected His own. People in this new movement-without-a-name that I see coming as a groundswell understand this and are tired of the striving and the artificiality of it all. They know that real prayer is found in a natural relationship that begins in the heart of a loving Father who draws us to Himself. By watching and hearing Jesus, His disciples—then and now—come to understand the Father's true heart.

Later on Jesus said, "I am the way, and the truth, and

the life; no one comes to the Father but through Me. If you had known Me, you would have known My Father also; from now on you know Him, and have seen Him" (John 14:6–7). He said this because the point was, and is, that you and I should come to know *Him*—Jesus—and through Him come into real relationship with the Father. We were created for intimacy with the Father. It's why He made us. Any teacher who places a layer of method between us and Him promulgates a false gospel, a new legalism based in human striving.

In Genesis 3 God came looking for Adam after he had sinned by eating from the tree of the knowledge of good and evil. God and Adam once walked together in the cool of the evening, enjoying one another's company, but sin shattered the relationship and disrupted their intimacy. Adam hid in the shame of his nakedness while God cried out in agony of grief, "Adam, where are you!" (See Genesis 3:9.)

So desperate was God the Father to restore that lost intimacy that He gave His only Son to die hideously on the cross to absolve the guilt, remove the barrier, and restore the connection. This prayer Jesus prayed—this *way* of prayer, if we catch the spirit of it—stands, therefore, as a marker, a signpost on the way to the kind of relationship Jesus had with His Father. A disciple becomes like his or her master. What Jesus had, we inherit.

It is important to understand that there's no such thing as King James Hebrew or King James Greek—the original language of Jesus's prayer is plain and simple. It's everyday stuff, *koine* Greek, common language, the Greek that people spoke daily in the streets. Informal and direct, this prayer comes to us in the language of simple intimacy.

When I call home from a ministry trip in a far country to talk to my wife, I don't say: "Greetings, O great and glorious spousal one! The radiance of thy presence surrounds me! Mine ears are warmed at the sound of thy resonant voice, and I long for thy touch. I beseech thee to think of me!" She'd wonder whether I'd either lost my mind or was seeing someone on the side! Accordingly the Lord's Prayer is direct, simple, warm, and human. In the coming move of God's Spirit, because we've become more human and down-to-earth, we will become more supernatural.

Jesus was trying to communicate the intimate and simple spirit of His relationship with His Father. This is part of the longing in the hearts of those called to a new day of freedom in the Lord.

"Our Father . . . "

Jesus began with, "Our Father who is in heaven" (Matt. 6:9). Every scholar I've studied knows that in the original Aramaic (a form of Hebrew) that Jesus and the disciples spoke on a daily basis, He taught them to address God as "Abba," the name by which a small child called his or her father.

Intimate, simple, and childlike, this prayer contains no formula. We're talking to Daddy, not learning to say the right things to make things happen. Wouldn't that be a form of salvation by works from which Jesus came to free us? Jesus prayed like a child on his daddy's knee in trust, love, and intimacy, and He taught us to do the same.

"HALLOWED BE YOUR NAME . . ."

I remember a time as a child when I stood in awe of my earthly father. I thought of him as the greatest saint in the world. Nobody could possibly have been more spiritual or more powerful than he. I knew that he was holy, and I thought he knew everything there was to know.

Jesus saw His Father in heaven like that and imparted that vision to His disciples (Matt. 6:9). It was like saying, "Here I am, Daddy. I am in awe of You. I know You are powerful and perfect and safe and clean, and there is no darkness in You."

It's almost a way of saying to God, "I can trust You," because holiness never varies. In holiness you find no shade of change. Holiness is goodness and perfect love all the time—love, joy, peace, patience, kindness, and self-control with never a hint of inconsistency. Because God is holy, therefore we can rest in Him, our Daddy, without fear. This is what Jesus wanted them to catch.

"YOUR KINGDOM COME . . ."

In Matthew 6:10 Jesus prayed, "Your kingdom come. Your will be done, on earth as it is in heaven." We could stop right there. In the kingdom of heaven the will of God comes to Earth. In the same way that in heaven every thought, every word, every impulse, and every desire of the Father instantly becomes reality, let it be so here.

The first goal of any prayer, therefore, must be to become attuned to the will of heaven, to discern and reflect the will of God in oneness with His heart. A key word for describing this would be *alignment.* The kingdom of God has much to do with aligning what happens on Earth and in us with the will and nature of heaven. When that alignment is in place, power flows.

This kind of alignment leads not to method but to relationship, to oneness with the Father's heart. If you cross the threads when you attach your garden hose, you've misaligned the connector. As a result there is no seal, you get a wet face, and water pressure is compromised! Or when the front wheels on your car are out of alignment, the tires wear down, and your car won't steer straight. "Your kingdom come" means, "Bring me (or us) into alignment with You, Father."

Most of the rest of the prayer flows from that single request. We see the will of heaven come to Earth when God provides for our daily needs as in, "Give us this day our daily bread" (v. 11). "Forgive us our debts, as we also have forgiven our debtors" (v. 12) reflects the will of heaven and the very nature of God.

Unforgiveness puts us out of alignment with God, so I want to pray, "Lord, forgive me, and I'll forgive those I need to forgive." If I fail in this, I will stand out of alignment with the power of heaven come to Earth. I'll miss connection with the kingdom of God ("Your will be done on earth as it is in heaven"). Power will be proportionately diminished because of hindered or broken relationship. Earth must align with heaven. I must align with God's heart.

"Do not lead us into temptation, but deliver us from evil" (v. 13). When we fall to temptation, we've fallen out of alignment with the flow of the power and nature of the kingdom and have stepped into an unclean stream that twists life and defiles relationships. We, therefore, ask to be delivered from the trap of temptation.

Deliverance from temptation has nothing to do with earning salvation. Salvation is a gift based on Jesus's sacrifice on the cross and has to do with how much God loves us and what He's willing to sacrifice for us. Jesus paid for it. The gift is free. It flows from God's holiness and perfect will imparted to us at the level of what and who we are and are becoming.

In reality, what many of us live and pray is actually, "My kingdom come. My will be done in heaven as it is on earth," with predictably disappointing results. We then are angry with God, become depressed, or have a pity party when God doesn't seem to bless self-centered prayers and lifestyles. He will not and cannot bless what fails to align with His goodness. While He does forgive and grant mercy for our failings, I'd rather have power and intimacy with Him than walk my own flawed path.

A LITTLE BIBLE HISTORY

As Moses's successor, Joshua inherited the task of leading the people into the Promised Land to conquer and occupy it. Toward that end he received both commands and promises:

> Every place on which the sole of your foot treads, I have given it to you, just as I spoke to Moses...No man will be able to stand before you all the days of your life. Just as I have been with Moses, I will be with you; I will not fail you or forsake you. Be strong and courageous, for you shall give this people possession of the land

which I swore to their fathers to give them. Only be strong and very courageous; be careful to do according to all the law which Moses My servant commanded you; do not turn from it to the right or to the left, so that you may have success wherever you go.

—JOSHUA 1:3–7

Certain instructions were given about preparing for this monumental task:

At that time the Lord said to Joshua, "Make for yourself flint knives and circumcise again the sons of Israel the second time." So Joshua made himself flint knives and circumcised the sons of Israel at Gibeath-haaraloth...Their children whom He raised up in their place, Joshua circumcised; for they were uncircumcised, because they had not circumcised them along the way. Now when they had finished circumcising all the nation, they remained in their places in the camp until they were healed.

—JOSHUA 5:2–8

Notice first that Joshua aligned himself with the will of God, observing the command, "Be careful to do according to all the law." He, therefore, led the people to circumcise themselves, as the mark of their covenant with God and as a symbol of cleansing away unrighteousness, before invading the Promised Land. So aligned, they obeyed the Lord's instructions for battle, and the walls of Jericho fell down (Josh. 6).

Later, in Joshua 7, they attacked the city of Ai and suffered a disastrous defeat. One man, Achan, was found to have hidden some of the forbidden booty from Jericho in his tent, and it was enough to put the nation out of alignment with the will and purposes of God. Power was accordingly diminished, and defeat at Ai followed.

Before the Day of Pentecost God breathed the Holy Spirit into the disciples to deal with sin. "So Jesus said to them again, 'Peace be with you; as the Father has sent Me, I also send you.' And when He had said this, He breathed on them and said to them, 'Receive the Holy Spirit. If you forgive the sins of any, their sins have been forgiven them; if you retain the sins of any, they have been retained'" (John 20:21–23).

The word *retain* means "seize and hurl." We have been given authority over sin to take hold of it and fling it from us. As we do so, we come into alignment with God's heart and nature. Character adjustments bring us closer to the image of the Son.

Following Jesus's ascension into heaven, the church held a ten-day prayer meeting in the Upper Room. As they acted upon what had been imparted in John 20, I believe whatever remained in their lives and hearts that failed to align with the flow of the kingdom of God was adjusted while they prayed. Then came the power that fell on the Day of Pentecost, followed by healings and deliverances.

Sometime later, in Acts 19, the sons of Sceva tried using the name of Jesus (whom they'd heard Paul preach) to cast out a demon. "And the evil spirit answered and said to them, 'I recognize Jesus, and I know about Paul, but who are you?' And the man, in whom was the evil spirit, leaped on them and subdued all of them and overpowered them, so that they fled out of that house naked and wounded" (Acts 19:15–16). The demon recognized a failure of alignment. It knew that the sons of Sceva had no real connection to Jesus. Their use of the name of Jesus therefore had no meaning and carried no authority.

DISCERNING PROPER ALIGNMENT

The thoughts of our hearts reveal the true state of our alignment and relationship with the Father. Likewise, my emotions often indicate what I have become attuned to. As the words that come out of my mouth reveal the condition of my heart, they tell the truth about my alignment as well.

Relationships serve the same revelatory purpose. For instance, do I relate to my spouse as Jesus does to His? Ephesians 5:25 says He loves His bride (the church, us) and gave Himself up for her. He laid down his life for her. She wounded Him then and she continues to do so today, yet He continues to love her, laying down His life and forgiving her again and again.

Is that *my* heart? Is my heart lined up with His in that way? If not, then the connection to power and blessing will be broken to some degree because when my earthly relationships in the body of Christ are broken, the likelihood is that my heavenly ones will be as well. I'm still saved and I'm still loved, but the kingdom of God is about God's will being done here in me just as it is in heaven. Shouldn't my prayer be aligned with the heart and will of God as they have been imprinted into me?

Another question to ask is, "Do I agree with God about myself, that I am royalty? That I am chosen?

Cleansed? Made holy by what Jesus has done? Forgiven?" This is part of proper alignment. When the threads of the connector between the pipes are crossed, power is proportionately diminished.

As a pastor, I've counseled couples in more broken marriages than I can count or remember. After all these years I'm still astounded at how professed Christians can so stubbornly hold on to issues and attitudes that clearly fail the test of alignment with God's heart. If this describes your own situation, then perhaps rather than cataloging the things you want done to your mate or telling God that you want out, try praying as Jesus did—aligned with the will of heaven: "Father, how do I align my heart with Yours? Yours never takes into account a wrong suffered. [See 1 Corinthians 13.] Your heart is all giving."

Then, rather than ask God to bless your unholiness and have it your way, ask Him to align you from the inside out with Him, which means, "to become conformed to the image of His Son" (Rom. 8:29). When Earth aligns with the will of heaven, power flows freely: "Your kingdom come. Your will be done, on earth as it is in heaven" (Matt. 6:10).

When Jesus faced the most difficult test of His life, hours before the cross and after pleading for another plan, He said in a true prayer of alignment, "Not My will, but Yours be done" (Luke 22:42). All of us have been saved because of this prayer and because of the power that resulted from it.

"Your kingdom come. Your will be done" is a prayer of submission, not direction. Not infrequently God stops me when I'm praying and tells me, "I don't need your directions." It's never God's way to align His will with mine. It can only work the other way around. I don't need to understand. Neither is it necessary for me to know what to say. My words don't move heaven. What does, rather, are my submission to the Father and a willingness to let Him cause my thoughts, my feelings, and my nature to conform to His.

We ask God for more power. We need that power for the sake of those who need healing in their bodies and breakthrough in relationships as well as signs, wonders, and miracles of provision. Alignment with the will of heaven is a major component of the thrust of the Lord's Prayer and the heart of what Jesus wanted the disciples to absorb.

Walking in the power of the kingdom and the presence of God won't be found in the method you learned at a conference or because you got the words right or because you followed the right steps. It comes from, "Our Abba...Your will here and now...just like in heaven." We access it through our submission to Him and from being in alignment with who He is and what He imparts into us as we become intimate with Him, learn to trust Him, and embrace the changes He sends. We must learn to allow Jesus to expose what isn't Him and establish in us what is Him as He aligns us with the will and the character of heaven.

The question is twofold: Do I trust Him enough for my heart to be one with His, and can I do that under the worst of circumstances, knowing that the outcome will be heaven come to Earth? This is the heart of the Lord's Prayer. It's a prayer of trust, submission, alignment: "I trust You for daily bread. Align my character by cleansing my sin. Align my character by cleansing my heart toward others who've wounded me. Align my character by taking the sin and brokenness out of me until I'm no longer so vulnerable to temptation or prone to harm others in any way."

This kind of holiness is so much more than, "Don't smoke, don't get stoned, and don't fornicate." It's how I react when my wife has a computer problem—again— and it's the thing I've told her how to deal with over and over—again—and I ask her if she did it, and she says she did—again—and I say, "No, you didn't, because if you had done it, then it would work." My anger and impatience rise—again—and pretty soon she's in tears—again.

At that point I know where my heart is out of alignment with God's. Consequently my prayers are hindered: "You husbands in the same way, live with your wives in an understanding way, as with someone weaker, since she is a woman; and show her honor as a fellow heir of the grace of life, so that your prayers will not be hindered" (1 Pet. 3:7).

I have just an hour to get something done that needs to happen for the sake of my job. If I don't get it done, there will be a price to pay; but my son needs me at the same time, and he can't wait. A choice lies before me, and which way I choose will tell me something of the state of my heart's alignment with the kingdom of God. On the basis of that choice, power will be released or diminished. God will love me either way. I'll still be saved either way because that's a gift, but power doesn't flow if the pipes aren't connected. Power flows best through things that look, feel, and resonate like God Himself.

When we come together to pray, are our relationships healthy? Are we aligned with God and one another? Am I one with my brothers and sisters? Am I thinking less than edifying thoughts about someone who is present to pray with the group? Whose agenda is it, mine or His? Is it the Father's heart in Jesus that informs my words, and does His heart infuse the spirit of those words when I speak them?

Do I need to be heard and seen by others as wise and gifted, or am I really in the humble heart of God? Jesus is the perfect and full revelation of the Father. In Matthew 11:29 Jesus says He is "humble in heart." The original Greek word means to stoop or to stoop low, to make oneself low. God humbles Himself, stoops low, to come to us. He abases Himself; He gets Himself dirty to come to us. One who is humble makes himself small in order to exalt others. That was Jesus, and it needs to be us, even in prayer.

Let our words spring from His heart. "Let Your kingdom come, Your will be done on Earth as in heaven; and let a part of that be that my inner self is aligned with Your will, forgiven and forgiving, cleansed, and delivered at the depths of who and what I am."

Finally, above all, as Jesus prayed in Matthew 6:13, let the Lord be glorified. "For Yours is the kingdom and the power and the glory forever and ever."

Chapter 12

WHAT KIND OF
CHRISTIANS ARE WE?

————◆————

What kind of Christians are we? That's a question we must answer as pressures mount in the world around us and as we feel them in our homes and daily lives. What, really, did we sign on for? Now that I'm in my sixties, I feel like Woodstock happened last year and the Jesus movement was yesterday. Inside I still feel a lot like I did back then, when I was a nineteen-year-old troublemaker destined to upset the culture around me.

As I reached my eighteenth year, the Jesus movement came into full flower. Hundreds of thousands of young people—hippies, nerds; it didn't matter—came streaming to Jesus. It became culturally cool to be Christian. There was no persecution and no opposition, except when we tried to join traditional churches where the traditional older people didn't like our style. Everywhere we went we carried our Bibles, like visible flags that advertised who we were. We attended Bible studies in meeting rooms at our high schools and in dorm rooms at college. We followed the latest Christian bands when contemporary Christian music was just being born and waited with bated breath for the next album to come out.

We evangelized in city parks and schools, shared our faith in classrooms, on campuses, and at work. No one opposed us. We used to say that you could stand on a street corner, shout Jesus, and a dozen kids would get saved. Thousands of us went off to Youth With A Mission's Discipleship Training School or trained with Youth for Christ so we could go forth to win the world.

In those days it seemed that being Christian was easy, something everyone respected. In the summer of my nineteenth year I went to a rock festival—a Woodstock wannabe—at Farragut State Park north of Coeur d'Alene, Idaho. They billed it as the Universal Life Church Picnic, and some foolish government officials believed that's what it was.

Concession stands sold drugs. Everywhere I looked I saw speed freaks in their twenties looking like eighty-year-olds. Marijuana smoke wafted over every campsite and filled the natural amphitheater where the bands played and hundreds of young people danced naked in the dust. Looking down from the rim of the amphitheater, it looked like the scene from that old Cecil B. DeMille movie *The Ten Commandments*, when the Israelites made the golden calf.

In the midst of all the sin and debauchery, one of the bands played a song in which the key lyrics went something like, "Well, hooray for the Jesus people! At least they know just where they're at!" It was easy to be Christian, and following Jesus was a cool thing to do.

We transitioned into adulthood in a time when the nation was prosperous. Yes, the war in Vietnam raged on, and even though a lot of us found ourselves drafted, the war was winding down and seemed a long way off. Passion for Jesus came easily. Society approved. Our peers smiled on us and were in it with us. Our parents who had prayed for revival for their children were thrilled.

THE IDEA OF LOVING JESUS

Here, however, lies a problem that some, perhaps many of us, fell into: as the movement simply swept us along, we were in love with the *idea* of being in love with Jesus. We jumped easily into the stream and felt a belonging, but somewhere in the midst of it a large percentage of us missed really being in love with Jesus Himself. Consequently, as life impacted us, many of us fell away or turned lukewarm.

You never know where you really are and what you really love until testing comes. You know whether you're in love with the idea of being in love with Jesus, rather than being in love with the real Jesus, only when life begins to fall apart and the culture turns against you. You begin to find out where you really stand when you face the prospect of losing your job because you spoke openly about your faith or stood for integrity for Jesus's sake.

You find out whether you're in love with the real Jesus, or merely the idea of being in love, when you own a bake shop and a gay couple brings a lawsuit against you because you didn't feel your Christian conscience would allow you to bake a wedding cake for a gay wedding. This happened in my city of Denver in 2012, and the bake shop owner lost the case.

You find out whether you're really in love with Jesus when the pressures begin to mount and you find you have some serious problems to solve in your marriage, or when your child in whom you've invested your life decides to abandon the foundation you gave him or her. At that point you find out whether it was just the idea or the real thing you've been in love with.

Will we really love Jesus when it no longer feels good to love Jesus? What are we really in love with? Are we in love with the benefits we believe He'll bring? Did we think He would solve all our problems? Did we expect Him to make us rich if we did and said the right things? Were we (or are we) only in pursuit of an amazing supernatural experience?

Maybe you thought He was supposed to plant you in a group of people who believe as you do, who never say or do anything wrong or offensive, who always treat you appropriately. Silly you! If you thought that, then please tell me what planet you're from.

REVIVAL DAYS

In 1994, after the Holy Spirit fell in Toronto, it became culturally cool among revival people to get blasted by the Spirit and fall, shake, laugh, and cry, "*Ho!*" Then it became the in thing to *act* like you were getting blasted by the Spirit and to fall, shake, laugh, and cry, "*Ho!*", whether or not God was really doing that. Movements can sweep you along like that! After a while, when the glow began to fade, some folks fell into depression and discouragement, as if God had let them down.

What were we in love with? Was it the experience of Jesus? Was it the style and the freedom? Or was it the real Jesus, no matter what He chose to send? When we began to be tested, where did all that love go? What happened to our passion?

When the signs and wonders flow and we see people being healed, hear angels' songs, and receive miraculous provision, love and passion are easy. It's easy to be in love with the *manifestations* of God, with the realization of His kingdom here on Earth, and mistake that for real love of Jesus Himself. Are we in love with all those things at the expense of being in love with the One who sends those things, whether or not He chooses to send them?

For instance, do I love my wife because she's beautiful and makes me feel good, or do I love her because she's her, no matter whether she remains those things over the years? Is it the image of a woman that I love, or is it the person she really is?

My mother and father, married for sixty-one years before my mother's death, grew old, stooped, and shriveled. My mother lost her mind to Alzheimer's disease and had to be confined to a nursing home for several years, yet still they loved. Even in my mother's final days they could be seen walking down the hall of the nursing home arm in arm, facing the most difficult time of their lives in unbroken covenant. After she died, my father said with tears of loneliness, "Even though her mind was broken, I could feel her spirit loving me, and now that's gone."

He wasn't in love with the idea of being in love. He wasn't in love because she remained youthfully beautiful or made him feel good. I remember clearly that she didn't always make him feel good, even in their younger years. He loved her because she was her, not for what she did for him. Can we learn this with Jesus?

THE FAITH OF THE EARLY CHURCH

Acts 2 reflects a time in the early church when the believers remained concentrated in Jerusalem. Luke described it this way:

> Day by day continuing with one mind in the temple, and breaking bread from house to house, they were taking their meals together with gladness and sincerity of heart, praising God and having favor with all the people. And the Lord was adding to their number day by day those who were being saved.
>
> —ACTS 2:46–47

In those early days they enjoyed favor from the surrounding population. It seemed as if everyone liked them, and as we experienced many years later in the Jesus movement, it was culturally good to be Christian.

Before very long, however, the first major missionary thrust out of Jerusalem developed, not because anyone grew passionate about going out to the mission field, but because the culture turned against them:

And Stephen, full of grace and power, was performing great wonders and signs among the people. But some men from what was called the Synagogue of the Freedmen, including both Cyrenians and Alexandrians, and some from Cilicia and Asia, rose up and argued with Stephen. But they were unable to cope with the wisdom and the Spirit with which he was speaking. Then they secretly induced men to say, "We have heard him speak blasphemous words against Moses and against God." And they stirred up the people, the elders and the scribes, and they came up to him and dragged him away and brought him before the Council.

—Acts 6:8–12

Stephen turned his defense before the council into an opportunity to declare the truth of who Jesus is. The response was vicious:

But they cried out with a loud voice, and covered their ears and rushed at him with one impulse. When they had driven him out of the city, they began stoning him; and the witnesses laid aside their robes at the feet of a young man named Saul. They went on stoning Stephen as he called on the Lord and said, "Lord Jesus, receive my spirit!" Then falling on his knees, he cried out with a loud voice, "Lord, do not hold this sin against them!" Having said this, he fell asleep.

—Acts 7:57–60

As always happens when people truly love Jesus, this attempt to stop the spread of the gospel only fed the fire and made it spread:

> But Saul began ravaging the church, entering house after house, and dragging off men and women, he would put them in prison. Therefore, those who had been scattered went about preaching the word.
> —ACTS 8:3–4

It became painful to be Christian. And still Stephen loved Jesus, not for a good feeling—being stoned to death is a definite negative—but simply for who Jesus is. No longer was it culturally cool to be Christian in Jerusalem. And when persecution scattered them, rather than going out discouraged or depressed, they went everywhere telling people about the One they loved.

POSING THE QUESTION

Having seen all this, are you in love with the *idea* of being in love with Jesus, or does real love for the real Jesus carry you through everything in life with passion and fire, even when the culture turns against you? Unless you're blind, you know the culture of our day has turned against us and that it will likely get worse.

Would you be able, as Peter and the other apostles were, to walk away from a flogging filled with joy? "So they went on their way from the presence of the Council, rejoicing that they had been considered worthy to suffer shame for His name. And every day, in the temple and from house to house, they kept right on teaching and preaching Jesus as the Christ" (Acts 5:41–42). Could you love Jesus when it's no longer easy to love Jesus, or do you love Him for the things He can do for you?

Those early Christians who so passionately loved Jesus held no delusions of cultural acceptance, promises of an easy road, or belief that God would make them prosperous. The crucifixion of Jesus remained fresh in their minds. Paul bore the scars for Jesus in his body. He, as well as the other early Christians, understood the cost:

> Are they servants of Christ?—I speak as if insane—I more so; in far more labors, in far more imprisonments, beaten times without number, often in danger of death. Five times I received from the Jews thirty-nine lashes. Three times I was beaten with rods, once I was stoned, three times I was shipwrecked, a night and a day I have spent in the deep. I have been on frequent journeys, in dangers from rivers, dangers from robbers, dangers from my countrymen, dangers from the Gentiles, dangers in the city, dangers in the wilderness, dangers on the sea, dangers among false brethren; I have been in labor and hardship, through many sleepless nights, in hunger and thirst, often without food, in cold and exposure. Apart from such external things, there is the daily pressure on me of concern for all the churches.
>
> —2 CORINTHIANS 11:23–28

In addition to the tortures he endured, Paul had to do much of his ministry from a jail cell. I personally believe that Paul was the likely author of Hebrews and that he therefore knew what he was talking about when he said: "Fixing our eyes on Jesus, the author and perfecter of faith, who for the joy set before Him endured the cross, despising the shame, and has sat down at the right hand of the throne of God. For consider Him who has endured such hostility by sinners against Himself, so that you will not grow weary and lose heart. You have not yet resisted to the point of shedding blood in your striving against sin" (Heb. 12:2–4). There couldn't have been one square inch of Paul's back that wasn't a mass of scars.

Both Jewish and Roman culture arrayed against them. It wasn't culturally acceptable to be Christian. Being a follower of Jesus exacted a price, and still they loved Him, even when it didn't feel good to do so. They understood that it might cost them their friends, their families, and, in some cases, their lives. They weren't crippled as we who live in America sometimes are by the delusion that they lived in a Christian nation. They knew they didn't.

The Jews hated them because they regarded them as a major threat to the historic faith, as they understood it. The Romans thought of them as troublemakers and atheists because they rejected the Roman gods. In the Roman world that kind of thing could collapse your business, get you fired, or get you killed. They knew what they faced. They knew what the cost would be, and still they persevered in real love for the real Jesus.

As I write, Pastor Saeed Abedini, an Iranian American from Idaho, languishes in an Iranian prison in danger of losing his life, having been beaten to the point of suffering internal injuries. The Islamic government of Iran arrested him after accusing him of working with the house churches there and of evangelizing. Pastor Saeed knows. He understands the wonder of loving the real Jesus, not the *idea* of loving Him, and he knows that it's worth it.

DESPERATE FOR REVIVAL?

Some of us are desperate to see revival. Are we in love with the idea of revival, or do we love the One who sends revival, loving Him for His own sake, no matter what happens to us? Are we hungry for signs and wonders, or are we desperate to know the One who sends signs and wonders? It's a subtle confusion that can overtake the best of us. I recall my father once sharing that the Lord had asked Him, "Which do you love more, John? Me, or the ministry you do *for* Me?" Some others of us need to hear it a different way: "Which do you love more, beloved? Me, or what I can do for you?"

People in Scripture said it in many varied ways. Moses pleaded for God's ways as the means of obtaining God's favor: "If I have found favor in Your sight, let me know Your ways that I may know You, so that I may find favor in Your sight" (Exod. 33:13). Above all else Moses wanted to know God's heart and character.

Paul wrote in Philippians 3:8, "More than that, I count all things to be loss in view of the surpassing value of knowing Christ Jesus my Lord, for whom I have suffered the loss of all things, and count them but rubbish so that I may gain Christ." It mattered little to him what he had or didn't have. He regarded suffering as a small price to pay for the wonder of really knowing Jesus, not the *idea* of loving Jesus.

If you love Jesus for the idea of loving Him and the pressure comes, you're finished. It's over, and you fall away. The glory of knowing the real Jesus carried Paul through everything he suffered.

As far back as 2007 I told my congregation that America as we have known it is done. I prophesied that we'd enter a period in which we would find out where our real faith lies. Would we discover that it is founded on a relationship with the real Jesus, or in prosperity and circumstances? A year later we entered the greatest recession since the Great Depression and the worst economic recovery on record. We've been tested, and it isn't over.

We live in a day when everything we believe is increasingly being despised. Our concept of morality has been labeled judgmental and hateful. Our faith is being written out of public life. We're being told where we can speak for Jesus and where we're not supposed to speak of Jesus. Increasingly there will be a price to pay for what we believe and for the God we know.

What kind of Christians are we? Is it the real Jesus we love, or is it the prosperity Jesus who is supposed to solve all our money woes if we just do the right things? Is it the healing Jesus who takes away all our pain so we never have to suffer again? Is it the Jesus who gives us a spiritual high? All those things are good and desirable, but they're not the real Jesus if that's what you're in love with.

Ultimately it comes back to Matthew 16:24–25: "Then Jesus said to His disciples, 'If anyone wishes to come after Me, he must deny himself, and take up his cross and follow Me. For whoever wishes to save his life will lose it; but whoever loses his life for My sake will find it.'" Heed the words of the apostle Paul in 1 Corinthians 15:31: "I affirm, brethren, by the boasting in you which I have in Christ Jesus our Lord, I die daily." He willingly embraced the sufferings that came his way so that he could "know Him and the power of His resurrection and the fellowship of His sufferings, being conformed to His death; in order that I may attain to the resurrection from the dead" (Phil. 3:10–11).

Is *that* the Jesus we're in love with? Can we love Him for who He really is? He'll do wonderful things. That will never stop, but can we get past the things He does, or the things we want Him to do, in order to truly know His heart? If we can, then I know we will see true revival in our day.

For example, in 1972 I chose a girl as my wife who happened to be a "babe"—but I didn't marry a babe; I married a woman. The babe, the hot girl, is an image that fades away with time, but the woman is a person—and the person is so much better than the babe long after she can't do for me those things that I thought were so wonderful in the beginning. The real Jesus—Jesus the real person—is infinitely better than all the other things we find to love *about* Him.

Conclusion

A PASTOR'S PROMISE

———◆———

I n this book I have spoken of the dissatisfaction and hunger that untold numbers of people have expressed to me. I share that hunger, magnified by the burden I carry not only for the same things I have felt for myself but also for the people I love.

There is more. We have been promised more. We cry out for more. We need more.

I have cried for a return to innocence and simplicity, having identified and rejected a host of legalistic layers and complications to our relationship with God that have accrued over many years. As the psalmist said, "I have been young and now I am old" (Ps. 37:25), and I have become ever more simple in my devotion to God the older I've become. Never have I been happier in Him.

Simplicity and trust are marvelous things, as are covenant faithfulness and good discipline. These have grown in me, but the Father's heart trumps them all. I want you to know Him for who He really is, and my prayer is that this book has served to help you grow in that knowledge. I could have written much more, but this has been the heart of it.

Several years ago the enemy spoke to me and said, "If you'll just tame things down and be 'nice,' I'll give you thousands." I knew what he meant. Tone down the preaching and water down the worship. Make "nice" and lighten up on the challenges. I told him no. Seeing thousands in the seats of my church would be nice, but I wouldn't trade the presence of the Lord for any degree of success. Neither will I cheat people that way. I'm called to make disciples.

I choose to preach a committed, passionate gospel for holiness and the transformation of lives. I refuse to hold worship down to a nice three songs. Nor will I present a tame, so-called seeker-sensitive, one-hour service that compromises my commitment to pursue passionate worship into breakthrough with God. I will take as much time as that breakthrough requires. I refuse to preach watered-down motivational sermons to make people feel good at the expense of the fullness of the truth of God's Word. I owe more than that to the people of a decaying culture that generates ever-increasing waves of human misery. I'm called to make disciples, not just fill the seats, and I will hold that course.

I choose to believe that a generation—largely but certainly not exclusively young—awaits the impartation of a purpose from the Father's heart to give their lives meaning and to galvanize a passion in their hearts for something greater than themselves. I realize this sets me, and those like me, apart from many others who share our years. (I'm sixty-two at this writing.) But I also know that Joshua and Caleb led a younger generation to take the Promised Land while in their eighties. My body may age, but youthfulness will always be a choice.

I choose to be a father to a fatherless generation and to lead my spiritual sons and daughters into their God-ordained destinies. I will love God's people with His own heart manifested through me, desiring to see them released in all they've been called to be. I will lead selflessly as God gives me aid to do so. I reject domination and control in all its forms.

I will do what I see my Father doing rather than cater to the culture around me, even as I speak in terms the culture can understand. I will obey my Savior's commands rather than cater to the felt needs of people. My Father knows them better than I ever will and loves them more.

I choose to look forward into the greater glory yet to be revealed rather than long for days and movements gone by, much less the Egypt from which my Savior freed me. Passing through the Red Sea was a wonderful experience, but it cannot compare with occupying the promise and living a destiny.

I choose to understand that grace is not permission to fail; rather, it calls me to and empowers me for a higher standard of love and holiness while also ensuring forgiveness when I fall short. I choose to understand hell is real and that Jesus is the only way, truth, and life given under heaven for those who would live eternally in paradise. There is no other sacrifice for sin. His written Word stands eternally true, and I will teach it faithfully. I owe it to a generation to stand for the truth.

These things I refuse to compromise. I will stand, and

having done all, I will stand, as did the saints before me. I may grow weary and I know I'll face opposition, even from those who would claim to be my brothers and sisters in faith, but I will not fall and I will not surrender. I have eternity before me. The enemy of my soul does not. I get to win. We together inherit the victory.

NOTES

———•———

CHAPTER 4
TWO PILLARS OF A FRUITFUL LIFE

1. Barna Group, "Most Twentysomethings Put Christianity on the Shelf Following Spiritually Active Teen Years," September 11, 2006, https://www.barna.org/barna-update/article/16-teensnext-gen/147-most-twentysomethings-put-christianity-on-the-shelf-following-spiritually-active-teen-years#.VIDJBNLF_wh (accessed December 4, 2014).

CHAPTER 5
YOU ARE THE LIGHT OF THE WORLD

1. US Department of Health and Human Services, National Center for Health Statistics, as reported in "Marriages and Divorce, 1900–2009," Information Please Database, http://www.infoplease.com/ipa/A0005044.html (accessed December 5, 2014).

2. Anthony Zurcher, "Report: US Prison Rates an 'Injustice,'" *Echo Chambers* (blog), BBC.com, May 2, 2014, http://www.bbc.com/news/blogs-echochambers-27260073 (accessed December 5, 2014).

3. Megan Brooks, "Information and Resources: Top 10 Most Prescribed, Top-Selling Drugs," WebMD.com, August 5, 2014, http://www.webmd.com/news/20140805/top-10-drugs (accessed December 5, 2014).

4. Centers for Disease Control and Prevention, "Suicide Prevention: Youth Suicide," January 9, 2014, http://www.cdc.gov/violenceprevention/pub/youth_suicide.html (accessed December 5, 2014).

EMPOWERED
TO RADICALLY CHANGE
YOUR WORLD

Charisma House brings you books, e-books, and other media from dynamic Spirit-filled Christians who are passionate about God.

Check out all of our releases from best-selling authors like **Jentezen Franklin**, **Perry Stone**, and **Kimberly Daniels** and experience God's supernatural power at work.

CHARISMA HOUSE

www.charismahouse.com
twitter.com/charismahouse • facebook.com/charismahouse